sweet booties!
AND BLANKETS, BONNETS, BIBS & MORE

LARK CRAFTS
Asheville

senior editor
Valerie Van Arsdale Shrader

editor
Nathalie Mornu

art director
Megan Kirby

illustrator
J'aime Allene

photographer
Sandra Stambaugh

cover designer
Megan Kirby

This book includes a CD that contains 12 PDF patterns for sewing many of the projects found in this book. The PDFs open with Adobe Reader. If you do not have Adobe Reader on your computer, visit http://get.adobe.com/reader/ for a free program download. For patterns that span two pages or more, simply print the pages you need on 8½ x 11 inch (21.5 x 28 cm) paper, align the pattern edges by matching the letters together (A with A, B with B, and so on), tape the pattern pieces together, then cut them out.

LARK CRAFTS

An Imprint of Sterling Publishing
387 Park Avenue South
New York, NY 10016

First Paperback Edition 2013
© 2008, Lark Books, an Imprint of Sterling Publishing Co., Inc.

ISBN 978-1-60059-315-4 (hardcover)   978-1-4547-0799-8 (paperback)

The Library of Congress has cataloged the hardcover edition as follows:

Sweet booties! : and blankets, bonnets, bibs, & more.
    p. cm.
  Includes index.
  ISBN 978-1-60059-315-4 (HC-PLC concealed spiral : alk. paper)
  1. Infants' clothing. 2. Sewing.
  TT637.S94 2009
  646.4'06--dc22

                                    2008018281

Distributed in Canada by Sterling Publishing
c/o Canadian Manda Group, 165 Dufferin Street
Toronto, Ontario, Canada M6K 3H6
Distributed in the United Kingdom by GMC Distribution Services
Castle Place, 166 High Street, Lewes, East Sussex, England BN7 1XU
Distributed in Australia by Capricorn Link (Australia) Pty. Ltd.
P.O. Box 704, Windsor, NSW 2756, Australia

For information about custom editions, special sales, and premium and corporate purchases, please contact Sterling Special Sales at 800-805-5489 or specialsales@sterlingpublishing.com.

Email academic@larkbooks.com for information about desk and examination copies. The complete policy can be found at larkcrafts.com.

Manufactured in China

2 4 6 8 10 9 7 5 3 1

larkcrafts.com

contents

introduction

Sure, there *might* be a few things sweeter than a baby, but you'll have to ponder real hard to come up with them. Think of a wee babe in a hand-stitched outfit. Now, that's sweet. Next, imagine it cooing away in a nursery decked out with handmade accessories. The sweetness factor just ratcheted up a few notches. Finally, picture that same baby drooling over the cutest hand-sewn toys. The sweetness level has blown off the charts. Don't even bother to try to think of anything sweeter. You might injure yourself.

Sewing up garments and accessories for Baby is a breeze. Most of the pattern pieces are so small it takes hardly more than two or three snips of the shears to cut them out, and the short little seams whiz through a sewing machine in just a second or so.

When you stitch up baby gear, it's an act of love. You're saying loud and clear, "Hey, Baby, I'm smitten! You deserve the best, and I'm gonna devote my precious time and creative resources to making you some little treasures!"

And this book has all kinds of great booty—literally. The opening chapter called Fun Afoot features six pairs of adorable footwear, and the following pages contain way more for you to stitch up. You'll find nifty hats, just the thing for keeping your wee one snug and warm. Baby may be little, but style matters big, so keep that cutie clean and chic during meals by whipping up an elegant bib like On the Town (page 68). Go for fun with cool soft toys like the Yo-Yo Mobile (page 92), a colorful cascade of easy-to-sew yo-yos to make Baby go gaga.

After a long day of eating, playing, and soaking in the compliments, help Baby wind down with a refreshing bath; we've got the perfect Bath Hoodie for drying off afterward (page 108). Sweet dreams are guaranteed among the handful of crib-sized quilts in the last section.

Besides embroidery, the 32 projects in this book feature all kinds of sweet, easy embellishment techniques, from patchwork and appliqué to ruffles. Can't remember how to do a particular technique? No problem: the first section of the book gives a refresher on things as diverse as embroidery stitches, making yo-yos, and mitering the binding on quilts.

So if you've fallen for an adorable baby—and which baby isn't?—this book has a wealth of things to whip up for that sweet young thing: teeny clothes, funky footwear, hip hats, plush toys, and the coziest of quilts...every project irresistible, just like Baby.

love that baby sew much...

This chapter gives you background on everything you need to know to sew the projects in this book, including sizing, materials, tools, and techniques. Novice sewers will find helpful information in this section. If you're experienced, glance at what's covered here in case you want to flip back and reference it later.

sizing info

Since infants grow like weeds, baby clothes are the ultimate hand-me-downs. It's usually a safe bet to sew up an item larger than you think you'll need. The garment may be too big today, but just wait a couple of weeks or months—it'll quickly become too small!

To buy extra wearing time, baby garments are frequently made from stretchy fabrics. They generally have growing room built in, too, and that roominess can be kept under control with elastic at the waist or legs. Besides, it's a lot easier to pop babies into something supple and roomy than to shimmy them into tight outfits.

When buying clothes for your bundle of joy, have you ever noticed how your three-month-old won't fit into a tiny T-shirt labeled for six months? Kids grow at different rates, so garment sizes frequently don't match a set standard. We've sized the clothing in this book by measurement rather than age. The sizes listed in the box at right serve as a guide; you know best the speed at which your little one is sprouting, and you should decide for yourself which size garment to make.

For many of the items in this book, we've provided full-size patterns in four different sizes. (In this case, the instructions will direct you to cut out *pattern* pieces.) Other garments were designed with a template that fits a specific size. Enlarge the templates in the back of the book by the percentage listed to get the intended size, then if you want to modify them, add or remove ¼ inch (6 mm) per size. For instance, the Hold Me Cloche on page 62 was designed as a size Large. If you want to make it in size Small instead (two sizes smaller), remove ½ inch (1.3 cm) from the sides of the hat template.

The fit of things like bibs, blankets, and toys doesn't matter, so the templates for those are one size fits all.

BOOTIE SIZES

Newborn: sole length of 4 ¾ inches (12 cm)
Small: sole length of 5¼ inches (13.3 cm)
Medium: sole length of 5 ¾ inches (14.6 cm)
Large: sole length of 6¼ inches (15.9 cm)

GARMENT SIZES

Newborn: 7 to 13 pounds (3.2 to 5.9 kg), 17 to 24 inches (43.2 to 61 cm)
Small: 13 to 18 pounds (5.9 to 8.2 kg), 24 to 26½ inches (61 to 67.3 cm)
Medium: 18 to 21 pounds (8.2 to 9.5 kg), 26½ to 31 inches (67.3 to 78.7 cm)
Large: 21 to 24 pounds (9.5 to 10.9 kg), 31 to 34 inches (78.7 to 86.4 cm)

HEADWEAR SIZES

Newborn: 17-inch (43.2 cm) circumference
Small: 18-inch (45.7 cm) circumference
Medium: 19-inch (48.3 cm) circumference
Large: 20-inch (50.8 cm) circumference

favored fabrics

The projects in this book call for a wide range of fabrics, chosen for very specific characteristics. Most important, consider the delicate nature of Baby's skin, and always select soft material; the more natural its fiber content, the better. Anything Baby comes into contact with is subject to staining, so look at the care instructions on the end of the bolt. Pick fabrics you can wash and dry without hassle and that will hold up despite numerous trips through the laundry.

Here's a quick rundown of some of the options you'll encounter. Always launder the fabric prior to beginning work; it's best to address shrinkage or lack of colorfastness before you spend time cutting and sewing.

terry cloth

Usually made of cotton, terry cloth is a sensible choice for baby items. Many varieties are super soft, making them ideal as backings for bibs or quilts. Besides, what could be easier to clean up with and wash than the fabric used to make towels? In fact, if you can't find terry at the fabric store, you can always cut up a towel and use it in a project.

fleece

Fleece and babies are meant to go together. Babies love the cuddly softness of fleece, and they look *so* cute wearing it. Fleece won't fall apart easily, it doesn't fray, and it's easy to wash, making it popular with parents, too. The Elf Caps (page 58) and Just Ducky booties (page 33) both call for fleece.

velour

Velour's most distinctive feature is a plush pile that feels and looks like velvet. The Birdie Rattles (page 80), made from knitted cotton velour, are irresistible to touch and hold. What more could you want for a baby toy?

felt

Like fleece, felt is a soft and cuddly nonwoven fabric that doesn't ravel or fray. Traditionally made from wool, synthetic felt is also available in a wide range of colors. Get the heavyweight type, not the thin squares designed for crafting. The Sweet Pea booties (page 30) are made entirely from felt, making them lightweight, durable, and functional. But did you even notice *that,* or did you simply spot how pretty they are?

cotton

Cotton's a smart choice (and comfortable for Baby). This natural fiber is easy to sew and available in a wide range of colors and prints. Although you may prefer 100 percent cotton, there's no harm in cotton-polyester blends, which may be just as soft and pretty, while shrinking less, wearing well, and requiring little ironing.

leather and suede

For durable booties that mimic real shoes, sewing with leather or suede (a napped, brushed leather) will do the trick. The Baby Janes (page 42) are made entirely of suede and felt, while the Snuggies (page 36) have suede soles. Many fabric stores sell scraps of leather and suede for next to nothing. You can run thin leather through a sewing machine just as if it were fabric; simply change the needle to one designed for sewing leather (any fabric store sells these). Other fabrics exist that mimic leather and suede, so you have plenty of options.

chenille

Chenille's a super-soft, textured fabric that can be made from wool, cotton, silk, or rayon. It can make an already soft and friendly item, like the Soft Blocks (page 97), into something deliciously cozy. Some chenille fabrics are more washable or fragile than others, so check out the details before you buy and test it before you sew.

stretch knit

Two clear advantages to stretch knit are that it's durable and has a lot of give, allowing Baby to squirm like a wiggle worm. Generally made from polyester, cotton, and/or wool combined with spandex, stretch knits are widely available. Use them to make the diaper covers on pages 86 and 94.

corduroy

Although corduroy's usually associated with pants, its cottony softness and durability make it a great choice for baby shoes. The variety of wale widths and its velvety, saturated color make it such a yummy fabric. Although babies don't walk around in their booties, it's nice to have something that looks and feels substantial on their feet.

ticking and canvas

Ticking is a strong, tightly woven fabric usually made from cotton or linen. It's commonly used to make mattress and pillow covers, but its durability and natural fibers make it a good option for booties as well. It's one of the fabrics used to make the Cruisers (page 39). Canvas is similar to ticking, in that it's made from natural fibers and is very durable.

found fabrics

When considering what fabrics to use for your projects, don't overlook the possibility of found materials. Thrift shops harbor all kinds of treasures just waiting to be recycled. Vintage tablecloths, curtains, and even dresses that are otherwise damaged or torn can provide plenty of usable fabric for a baby outfit, toy, or hat. Even small sections of piecework from otherwise unusable quilts can be incorporated into something like the Quilted Bib (page 72). Sweaters, too, are a great material source, as in the No-Knit Hat (page 49).

fusible web

A synthetic material called fusible web is used in a number of the projects. Available in different weights, the web is placed between two fabrics and then pressed with an iron. The heat melts the web and fuses the two fabrics together.

Don't be fooled into thinking that heavier weights of fusible web adhere better; to avoid overkill and fusible web soaking through a fabric, err on the side of testing lighter weights first on the fabric you plan to use. Make sure that your iron never directly touches the web or it will melt onto the iron, leaving a mess that doesn't clean up with baby wipes.

Fusible web is available in a number of forms and is commonly sold by the yard in rolls of varying widths. The kind recommended for the projects in this book is paper-backed fusible web, which is ideal for appliqué. Check out page 25 to learn how to use it for this nifty embellishment technique.

battings and fillers

When a project calls for stuffing, polyester fiberfill is the best choice, mainly because it's washable. The grade one variety not only keeps its shape well but is also resilient, nonallergenic, and readily available in craft and sewing stores. Grade two is coarser, has more bounce than grade one, and is more environmentally friendly, but it's usually only available in bulk.

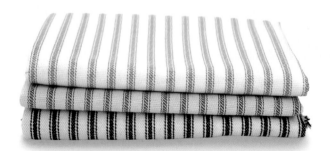

choosing embellishments

Because babies experience the world through their mouths, they pop everything that'll fit right inside it. Punkin's safety is your number one priority, so keep a couple of things in mind when making stuff for a baby.

Avoid embellishing with small items that might come loose and get swallowed. Sew buttons on securely, or consider using snaps instead. Properly installed snaps should stay on for good, and they come in pretty finishes and colors.

Appliqués (page 25) are the perfect embellishment because you can use any motif you like, and since they're sewn down on all sides, there's no way they'll come off. Ruffles are sweet and sewn down, too. Bias tape finishes off an edge neatly while adding emphasis to it. Make tassels and pom-poms fairly large, and stitch them on carefully with yarn. Yo-yos (page 25) are so, so cute, but make sure they won't come off.

materials and tools

All the projects in this book call for the Sewing Kit in the box below, so gather these items before you start. Chances are you have all of the supplies on this list right in your sewing basket, or not too far away. Fabric remnants, extra buttons, and leftover trim and yarn may all come in handy, too.

SEWING KIT
- Sewing scissors or shears
- Craft scissors
- Pinking shears (optional)
- Rotary cutter, mat, and ruler
- Sewing machine and needles
- Hand-sewing and embroidery needles
- Straight pins
- Safety pins
- Seam ripper
- Iron and ironing board
- Thread to match your project
- Embroidery floss (as needed)
- Tape measure
- Water-soluble fabric marker
- Scrap paper (for templates)
- Pencil with an eraser

---

scissors and shears

What's the difference between scissors and shears? Shears are larger, usually 7 to 12 inches (17.8 to 30.5 cm) long, and they have one larger finger hole. Sharp, quality scissors or shears are *so* worth the investment. They'll last a long time and make a noticeable difference when cutting fabric. Never use your sewing scissors for cutting paper! The paper fibers quickly dull the blades, making them useless for cutting fabric.

Sewing usually involves paper templates or patterns. For cutting these, reserve a pair of cheap scissors of short to moderate length to make fine cuts on pattern curves and corners.

One option for finishing raw edges is to cut out fabric with pinking shears. Pinking results in a serrated edge that doesn't fray as easily as a straight-cut raw edge does. Bonus: It looks mighty pretty.

rotary cutters

A rotary cutter cuts clean, straight lines in no time flat. If you've never used one, you'll wonder, "Hey, baby, where you been all my life?" You use this tool with a cutting mat, which protects both the blade and the table you're cutting on. A transparent ruler with grid lines makes it easy to line up straight edges.

To make a cut, hold the cutter at a 45° angle, making sure the blade is set firmly against the ruler's edge. Keep an even pressure on the cutter, and always cut away from yourself. The blade is razor-sharp, so make sure your fingers aren't too close to the edge of the ruler when you cut—and always keep the guard over the blade when you're not cutting.

Don't use a rotary cutter on fake fur or furry fleece; you'll end up with fur all over the place. For these fabrics, it's best to stick with scissors and cut through just the backing fabric, not the fur itself. It's a little more work, but a lot less mess.

sewing machine

Most of the projects in this book require a sewing machine. You should know its basic operation, such as zigzagging and adjusting the stitch length and stitch tension for different fabric thicknesses, but you won't have to do anything fancy like installing zippers or making a buttonhole. What could be easier?

Two projects—the Beautiful Bloomers (page 94) and Under Cover (page 86)—suggest using a serger, but you can make both diaper covers without a serger by finishing the raw edges using a more standard method, such as a double-fold hem (page 20).

pins and needles

You may break your sewing machine needle when sewing through many thicknesses of fabric, or if you nick a lot of pins while sewing, the needle will dull. Sewing machine needles are cheap, so keep extras on hand. It's a good rule of thumb to start each sewing project with a new needle. A couple of these projects are made of stretch knits, which require a ballpoint needle. These round-tipped needles push between the fabric fibers rather than piercing them, which can cause a run or pull in the weave of a knit.

Some projects involve a bit of hand sewing to close an opening or attach a button. A variety pack of needles will include every type you need. Choose a finer needle for lightweight fabrics and a thicker, longer needle for heavier fabrics. Use a ballpoint needle for knit fabrics. If you like adding patches of embroidery, use an embroidery needle. This needle has a longer eye for ease in threading multiple strands of floss at once, although it can be used for regular hand sewing as well.

Finding it challenging to thread the needle? Get a needle threader—a fine loop of wire attached to a small holder. This optional tool is very handy. Just push the stiff wire effortlessly through the eye of about any needle, insert the thread in the resulting wire loop, and when you pull the wire back through the needle, it carries the thread back with it, threading the needle. *Voilà!*

When it comes to straight pins, short metal pins with tiny heads will do the job for these projects. However, longer pins with plastic or glass heads are easier to handle and easier to see. Don't forget to also have plenty of safety pins on hand, in different sizes. You'll need them when it's time to thread some elastic or a drawstring through a casing.

threads and flosses

Please resist the three-for-a-dollar bargain bin thread. It knots and snags in sewing machines, so it's much smarter to buy quality thread for trouble-free stitching and a stronger, longer-lasting seam. You're investing your valuable time on a priceless creature, so why skimp on thread?

Select thread just a shade darker than your fabric. When sewing with stretchy fabrics, use polyester or cotton-wrapped polyester thread, both of which have some give. For cotton or other natural fibers, 100 percent mercerized cotton thread is the best choice.

If you want to experiment with decorative, hand-sewn details, use embroidery floss, a decorative thread that comes in six loosely twisted strands. It's available in cotton, silk, rayon, and other fibers, in a vast array of colors for every needlework application. Several strands can be used at once with an embroidery needle for sewing decorative stitches. The Best Friends blanket (page 106) is a good project for trying out your ideas.

ironing tools

Don't underestimate the power of an iron and a good ironing surface. You'll need these to press open the seams around tight curves and corners. It makes all the difference in producing a neat little pair of booties or a hat with crisp edges. If you don't have a steam iron—or even if you do—it's also handy to have a little spray bottle filled with water to soften stubborn wrinkles.

Some of the project instructions tell you to finger press. That means you should not use an iron because it could damage the fabric. Instead, rub your finger along the inside of the seam to open it up.

seam ripper

We all make mistakes, and it's much faster to undo them with the indispensable seam ripper. You can also use this tool to open up the ends of a casing (for elastic or a drawstring) or pick apart a line of embroidery that's too tight or in the wrong place—or maybe you just changed your mind.

sewing techniques

You don't need any fancy skills for making these projects, but a refresher course on the basics won't hurt. Here's the rundown on a few techniques that come in handy.

selected stitches

As you already know, most machine stitches are easily adjusted by redialing the length, from a loose basting stitch to a regular stitch to a tight stitch. You can also change the width to make a zigzag stitch. It's a good idea to test different lengths and widths on the fabric you'll be using, especially if you're sewing with fleece or other thick or textured fabrics. Some basic machine stitches you'll come across are defined below, and so are some simple hand stitches.

RUNNING STITCH

The running stitch just scoots across the material. Simply weave your needle in and out of the fabrics, keeping the size of the stitches as uniform as you can (figure 1).

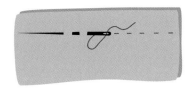

figure 1

TOPSTITCH

Topstitching shows on the top or right side of the fabric, as opposed to being hidden in a seam. This machine stitch is commonly used along necklines, hems, or other seams to tack a facing or seam allowance in place. It can be decorative by being sewn with contrasting thread and sewn in one or more parallel lines.

BLIND STITCH

This stitch is invisible. Working from right to left, make a small horizontal stitch that picks up just a thread of one of the fabrics; ¼ inch (6 mm) to the left, pick up a thread of the other fabric. Repeat, alternating between fabrics (figure 2).

figure 2

BASTING STITCH

Basting temporarily secures two edges of fabric where a seam is intended to go. This stitch is the same as a running stitch, but with very long stitches that are easily removed later.

WHIPSTITCH

Whipstitch is a hand stitch used for binding edges to prevent raveling; it also sews edges together very tightly. Working from the wrong side, insert the needle perpendicular to the fabric edge, over and over and over again (figure 3). The stitches will be slanted.

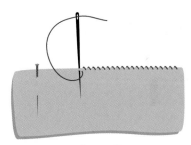

figure 3

EDGESTITCH

This stitch is pretty much what it sounds like—machine stitching along the edge of one fabric piece.

savvy seams

Finish your seams as you wish, with pinking shears or by sewing a zigzag stitch close to the edge. Both methods keep the raw edges of the seam from raveling.

making a double-fold hem

For finishing a raw edge, like the bottom of the Oh, Kimono (page 84), the most straightforward solution is a double-fold hem. The hem can be as wide or as narrow as you wish, but for baby garments, you'll probably want a very narrow one. Fold the edge ¼ inch (6 mm) to the inside and press it, then fold it another ¼ inch (6 mm) and press again. Stitch in place. (If you're in a hurry and the fabric cooperates, you don't need to press it each time. But at the very least pin the fold in place and check that it's even all the way around before you stitch.)

clipping curves and corners

When you sew a seam that curves outward, such as bootie toes, all the material on the curve bunches together when you turn the bootie right side out. To help the fabric find its own space and lay flat, make little V-shaped notches about two-thirds of the way into the seam allowance in several places on the curve (figure 4). This allows the fabric to overlap slightly where it was snipped and results in a smoother curve and seam on the right side.

The same dynamic applies to an inside curve, like the neckline around a bib. In this case,

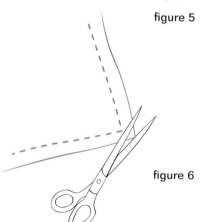

figure 4

making straight clips in the curve allows the seam to spread out when turned (figure 5). Otherwise, you'll get puckering all along the seam.

In a similar fashion, when a stitched corner is turned right side out, all that fabric has nowhere to go and the corner puckers in on itself. Before turning anything with a corner, such as a baby blanket or a burp cloth, clip straight across the corner of the seam allowance, halfway between the stitching and the corner of the fabric (figure 6). Cutting too close to the stitching weakens the corner, so be careful. Use the eraser end of a pencil or a chopstick to push out the corners, and press them to set the shape. You can then topstitch to keep the corners tidy.

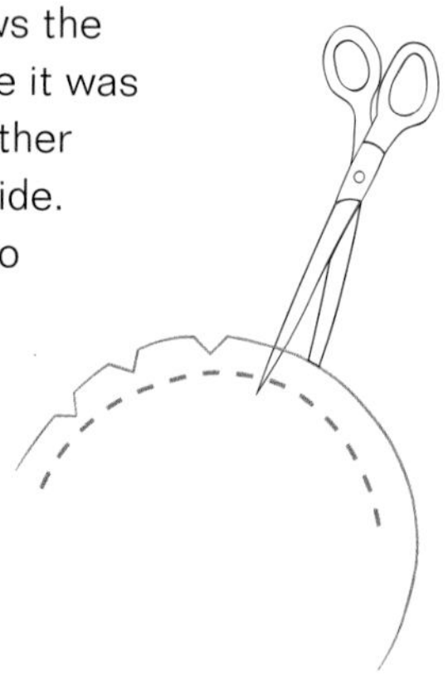

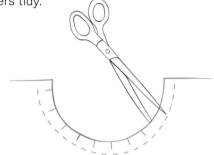

figure 5

figure 6

making a casing

Some of the projects call for either elastic or a drawstring, and that means making a casing. The process is pretty much the same as for a double-fold hem. Start by folding under the edge of the fabric ¼ inch (6 mm) or less. The next fold is determined by the width of the elastic or tie you plan to use. If you're using ½-inch (1.3 cm) elastic, make the next fold that width plus about ⅛ inch (3 mm). This gives you some wiggle room for inserting the elastic, usually with the help of a safety pin attached to one end (figure 7), and gives the elastic some breathing room. Don't add too much extra, though, or the elastic can twist in the casing—even non-roll elastic doesn't always behave.

For a drawstring, you can double or triple the width of the second fold. Twisting isn't an issue with a drawstring, and the gathers look nicer if the casing isn't too narrow or tight.

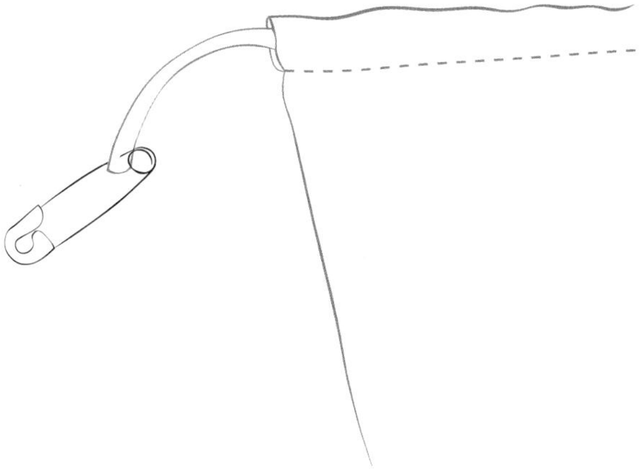

attaching hook-and-loop tape

Hook-and-loop tape is the handiest of fasteners for baby garments. Who wants to fuss with buttons and snaps when trying to feed a hungry, squirming baby? The tape is easy to apply when you sew, too, with just a couple of pointers to keep in mind.

The main thing is to buy the right kind of hook-and-loop to begin with. The little precut dots and squares look tidy and simple to apply, but their adhesive backings may not hold up through the wash. And if you try to stitch them after sticking them on, the adhesive will gum up and ruin your needle. It's better to use the tape that comes in rolls or strips and cut it to the size you need.

When attaching hook-and-loop to bibs, it's easy to get mixed up about the overlapping flaps that go behind the baby's neck. Put one side (the hook or the loop) on the *back* side of a flap and the other side on the *top* of the opposite flap (figure 8). Always check that the closures line up before stitching the tape down.

figure 7

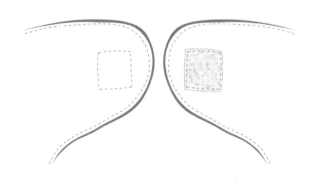

figure 8

working with bias tape

Bias tape is a narrow strip of fabric that's been cut on the bias (at a 45° angle to the grain) to give it more stretch. It's then folded and pressed in one way or another. You can buy single-fold or double-fold bias tape in a variety of colors, and in widths from ¼ inch to 3 inches (6 mm to 7.6 cm). Because it gives, or stretches, bias tape is ideal for finishing curved raw fabric edges that are impossible to turn and hem, such as the long curves around the neckline of a bib. Plus, it gives a crisp, finished look.

Double-fold bias tape has been folded and pressed down the center, and then both sides have been folded and pressed toward the center fold. This is the perfect solution for enclosing a raw edge—just slip the raw edge between the folds of the tape, pin everything together, and stitch the tape in place.

There's a handy little trick to this, though. When you look closely at the double-fold tape, you'll notice the folded edges aren't exactly the same width. The idea is to pin the narrower fold on the right side of the fabric with the wider fold in back. When you stitch along the top, you'll automatically catch the back. This makes things so much easier!

QUICK AND EASY STRAPS

It's a snap to make straps with double-fold bias tape. Just stitch together the long edge of a folded strip, and you've got a straight, tidy little strap with finished ends. Use it for ties on a bib or kimono.

making mitered corners

Another classic use of bias tape is finishing off the edges of quilts, as on the Cuddle Quilt (page 118). Quilt binding strips are typically at least 1 inch (2.5 cm) wide. When working with one long strip of bias tape, mitering is a great way to handle the corners. Here's how it's done:

1. Lay the quilt down, right side facing up. Beginning along on one side, open up the binding and lay it flat, right side down. Line up the binding's edge with the edge of the quilt. Start stitching 1 inch (2.5 cm) from the beginning of the binding (so you can attach it later to the other end) and sew ¼ inch (6 mm) from the edge. When you near a corner, stop ¼ inch (6 mm) from the corner.

2. Open up the binding and fold the fabric straight up and away from the quilt, forming a crease that points to the corner at a 45° angle (figure 9).

3. Keeping the angled fold in place, turn the binding back down to align with the edge of the quilt (figure 10). Continue stitching ¼ inch (6 mm) from the edge.

4. Repeat as you bind the other corners. When you come back around, stop sewing a few inches short of your starting point. Carefully trim the binding to overlap the beginning by 1¼ inches (3.2 cm). Fold the short edge under ¼ inch (6 mm) and press. Place the folded end of the binding under the beginning of the binding (the inch you left unsewn earlier) to encase it.

5. Continue stitching ¼ inch (6 mm) from the edge until you return to the starting point. Clip the corners (page 20) and turn the binding to the back side of the quilt. Press, making sure there's still a fold of binding on the front side (figure 11).

6. Blind stitch by hand (page 19) all the way around the back side of the quilt for a seamless finish. If you prefer, topstitch around close to the inside edge of the quilt binding for a different look.

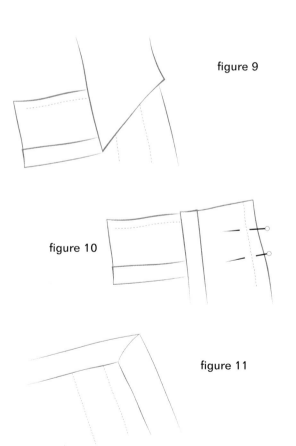

figure 9

figure 10

figure 11

embellishment techniques

Add flair and distinction to Baby's wardrobe and accessories with these charming methods of ornamentation.

making appliqués

Appliqué is French for "this is rrreally cool!"—just kidding. Appliqués are shaped pieces of cloth applied to the surface of another fabric. Use paper-backed fusible web to add these irresistible details.

1. Select a shape, such as the flowers for the Sweet Peas booties (page 30). Use a permanent marker to trace the shape on the paper side of the fusible web. Some designs, such as the letter "b" in Crib Notes (page 110), need to be traced in reverse so the end result will be oriented correctly.

2. Roughly cut around the traced shape, on the lines. Follow the manufacturer's instructions to adhere the shape to the wrong side of the appliqué fabric.

3. Cut out the shape along the lines. Remove the paper backing and adhere the shape to the selected background fabric with an iron. Use a zigzag stitch along the edge of the shape to secure it to the fabric and minimize fraying.

making yo-yos

A traditional project for little kids just learning to sew, yo-yos are puffy little fabric rosettes to use as embellishments or stitch together into quilts, vests, and all sorts of things. They're quick, easy, and fun to make.

1. Cut a fabric circle in the size given in the instructions.

2. Fold the edge back ¼ inch (6 mm) while hand sewing a running stitch close to it (figure 12). After stitching completely around the circle, leave a long tail when you cut the thread.

3. Gently pull the thread to gather the perimeter of the circle (figure 13) and flatten the yo-yo.

If you want to make a lot of yo-yos at once (say you feel ambitious and want to make a dozen Yo-Yo Mobiles [page 92] as holiday gifts), you might consider looking online or in quilt shops for a yo-yo maker, a tool that guides the placement of your running stitches to help you whip up yo-yos faster and more accurately.

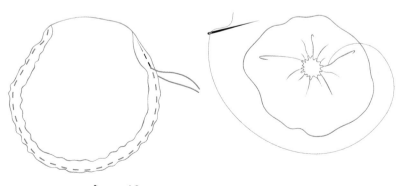

figure 12

figure 13

tassels and pom-poms

These bouncy, fringy embellishments are as fun to look at and touch as they are to make.

1. Cut a rectangle out of a scrap of cardboard; you'll be given the size to make it in the instructions.

2. Wrap yarn around it as many times as directed. Slip a separate piece of yarn under one side and tie it tightly around the pieces (figure 14). Slide the yarn off the cardboard and cut the opposite side.

3. Wrap another piece of yarn around the tassel and tightly tie it about ¾ inch (1.9 cm) down from the first tie. Trim any uneven ends.

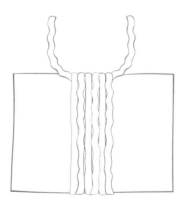

figure 14

gathering ruffles

Why go plain when you can add row upon row of frills? A gathered edge or a ruffle—such as those on Beautiful Bloomers (page 94) and Ring Around (page 89)—is easy to achieve.

1. Run two parallel lines of basting stitches along the edge you want to gather, leaving long ends when you cut the machine threads.

2. Pull both of the long threads from one side only (make sure not to pull them completely out!), pushing the fabric across them in the opposite direction (figure 15) until it's the right length, then distribute the gathers evenly across it.

3. Leave the basting threads in place as you pin and stitch the ruffle to the intended fabric, and then gently remove them.

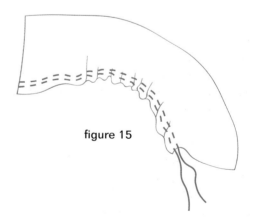

figure 15

making bias tape

Sometimes you just can't find bias tape in the right color. Other times, what you really want is binding made from a print to coordinate with the other fabrics you used. If you're willing to spend just a little extra time, you can make the binding yourself.

1. Decide how wide you want the finished binding to be. Multiply that by four, and cut several strips that width on the bias (figure 16). For example, to make finished bias tape ¼ inch (6 mm) wide, cut bias strips 1 inch (2.5 cm) wide.

2. Stitch the strips end to end until you have one strip long enough to cover the raw edge you have in mind. Trim the seam allowances and press open. (If you're ambitious, try for a professional look and stitch the strips together on the diagonal [figure 17]. It's tricky, but it distributes the bulk of the seam rather nicely.)

3. Fold and press the entire length of the strip right down the middle. Open up the strip and fold each of the sides in toward the pressed center line (figure 18). If you can manage it, make one side slightly wider than the other. Press the side folds, then refold on the center line and press again (figure 19). For tapes ½ inch (1.3 cm) or wider, you can adjust the width of the side folds for less bulk.

If you like the look of custom bias tape and want to make it frequently, there's a real time-saver of a tool available in sewing stores and online. After you make the flat strips, you pull them through this folding device that allows you to press all three folds at once.

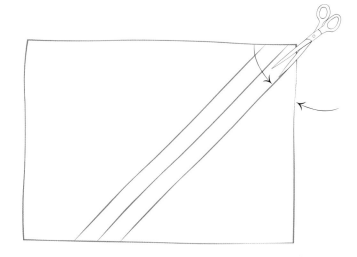

figure 16

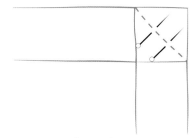

figure 17

figure 18

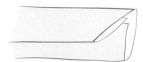

figure 19

embroidering

Although most of the projects in this book are stitched with a sewing machine, every now and then you'll want or need to sew something by hand. The projects in this book call for only a few types of embroidery stitches, which are illustrated here.

BLANKET STITCH
Both decorative and functional, the blanket stitch accentuates an edge or can attach an appliqué to a layer of fabric (figure 20).

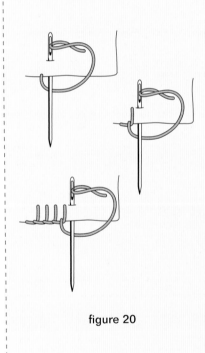

figure 20

LAZY DAISY STITCH
This method is used to stitch in a circle to form a flower (figure 21).

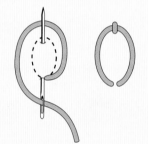

figure 21

SATIN STITCH
The satin stitch is composed of parallel rows of straight stitches, often to fill in an outline (figure 22).

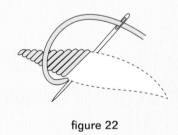

figure 22

Now that you have all the background information you need, it's time to get to the real reason you picked up this book: to make all kinds of cute, tiny things to lavish on the poopsie. So what'll it be first? A soft blankie for swaddling that dreamy little creature, or a floppy hat to keep away the rays? Rattles to hang from the crib—maybe a bib and burp cloth set that keeps everyone tidy? It's all here. You ready to sew for Baby? You bet your sweet bootie!

the projects

sweet peas

Whether tiptoeing through the tulips or watching Mama garden, your baby girl will look adorable in these darling slippers. They're made from soft and cuddly felt with sweet touches of embroidery and a ribbon tie.

what you need

Sewing Kit (page 15)

1 piece of 6 x 9-inch (15.2 x 22.9 cm) felt for the outside top

2 pieces of 6 x 9-inch (15.2 x 22.9 cm) felt in a complementary color

Scraps of colored felt for the flowers

Matching or contrasting embroidery floss

Paper-backed fusible web, 3 x 6-inch (7.6 x 15.2 cm) scrap

1 yard (91.4 cm) of ribbon for the ties

Small hole punch

seam allowance

⅛ inch (3 mm)

pattern pieces

top

sole

flower

flower center

designer: **Joan K. Morris**

what you do

1. Using the pattern, cut two top pieces from the single piece of felt. Cut two top pieces and two bottom pieces from the felt that's a complementary color. Cut two flowers and two flower centers from the scraps of colored felt.

2. Pin two top pieces of different colors together. With the embroidery floss and needle, hand sew a blanket stitch (page 28) along the top edge and around the circular cutout of both pieces (figure 1). Repeat for the other pair of tops.

3. At the back of the heel, overlap the two edges by ⅛ inch (3 mm) and hand sew them together with a blanket stitch (figure 2). Repeat for the other bootie top.

4. Machine baste each set of toes together. With the booties turned inside out, pin the soles in position and gather the basting to ease the front so the sole fits (figure 3).

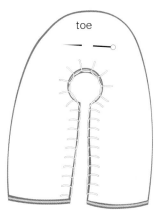

figure 1

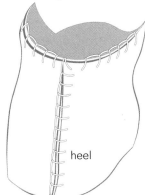

figure 2

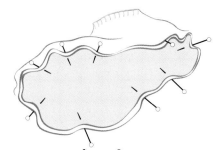

figure 3

5. Stitch ⅛ inch (3 mm) from the edge around each sole and bootie top. Clip the curves (page 20) and turn each bootie right side out.

6. Using the hole punch, make holes in the corners of each bootie and sew a blanket stitch around them for reinforcement.

7. Cut the flower shapes from both the felt and the paper-backed fusible web, using the pattern as a guide. Following the manufacturer's instructions, use the fusible web to adhere two large flowers together; the double thickness will give it some strength. Adhere the other pieces as shown.

8. Use the embroidery floss and the lazy daisy stitch (page 28) to attach the flowers to the booties.

9. On each bootie, run 18 inches (45.7 cm) of ribbon from the outside of one hole through the inside of the other and tie a bow.

When Baby's wearing these, she'll be ready to star in her own fairy tale.

just ducky

Cold tootsies? Slip little feet into these plush fleece booties and they'll be snug as a bug. The inspiration for this project is all in the fabric. In cheery yellow and bright orange, they look like they were colored with crayons.

what you need

Sewing Kit (page 15)

¼ yard (22.9 cm) of fleece

¼ yard (22.9 cm) of cotton fabric for lining

Small piece of hook-and-loop tape

seam allowance

⅜ inch (1 cm)

pattern pieces

top

sole

what you do

1. Using the pattern, cut two boot tops and two soles from both the fleece and the lining fabric. Transfer the dots from the boot top pattern to the fleece and lining pieces.

2. Cut two 10 x 2½-inch (25.4 x 6.4 cm) rectangles from the lining fabric to serve as straps. Fold each rectangle in half lengthwise. Press flat. Open them up and fold each side in toward the crease down the center and press. Refold down the original crease and press again (figure 1).

3. Lay one strap across the top of a fleece boot piece. The top of the strap should be 1¼ inches (3.2 cm) down from the top edge of the boot piece. Place one end of the strap flush with the front of the boot. Allow the other end to hang off the front—it's the strap that will wrap around the front of the finished boot. On that end, use a water-soluble pen to mark ½ inch (1.3 cm) from the edge of the boot front. Topstitch the strap on the top and bottom, stopping at the mark you made (figure 2). Repeat for the other fleece boot, making sure that the strap is hanging off the opposite side.

figure 1

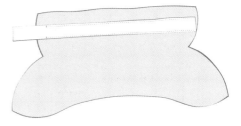

figure 2

designer: **Wendi Gratz**

figure 3

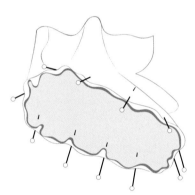

figure 4

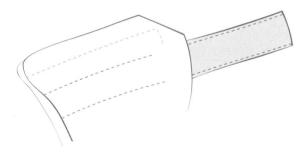

figure 5

4. Fold each boot piece—fleece and lining—in half, right sides together, and pin. Stitch from the dot down to the sole. Backstitch at the beginning and end of the seam. Snip to the marked dot at each corner (figure 3).

5. Pin the fleece soles to the lining boot tops, and the lining soles to the fleece boot tops (figure 4). Stitch all the way around each.

6. Keep the boot linings wrong side out. Turn the fleece boots right side out and tuck each one inside a lining boot. Align the top edges and open sides, and pin. Start stitching just below the short end of the strap. Stitch up the side and across the top. Turn the corner and stitch a short way down the other side, stopping short of the long end of the strap. Clip the fabric at the stitched corners (figure 5).

7. Pull the fleece boot from inside the lining boot, through the unsewn part at the front of the boot. Tuck the lining down into the fleece boot. Sew up the rest of the front by hand. Repeat with the other boot.

8. On the loose end of the strap, turn the raw end under ¼ inch (6 mm) and sew a small square of the hook-and-loop tape over the raw edge. Wrap the strap around the front of the boot and topstitch a corresponding square of hook-and-loop tape where the end of the strap lands (figure 6). Do the same with the other boot.

Slip on Baby's feet and watch them kick with glee.

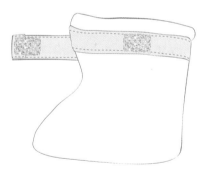

figure 6

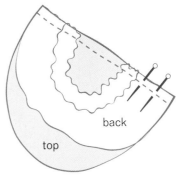

snuggies

Go ahead, Baby, kick off your socks. You won't need them with the ultra-soft fleece lining in these comfy booties. Want to go outside? No problem—with their sturdy suede souls, these booties are made for walking.

what you need

Sewing Kit (page 15)

20-inch (50.8 cm) square of cotton or corduroy for the outer fabric

20-inch (50.8 cm) square of fleece for the lining

10-inch (25.4 cm) square of suede or slip-proof material for the soles (optional)

Glue stick

10 inches (25.4 cm) of ⅜-inch or ³⁄₁₆-inch (1 cm or 5 mm) elastic

seam allowance

⅛ inch (3 mm)

pattern pieces

top

back

sole

designer: **Katherine Accettura**

what you do

1. Cut out the pattern. For all pattern pieces, cut two from the outer fabric and cut two from the fleece. Cut two soles from the suede or slip-proof material.

2. For the soles, pair the outer fabrics with the fleece linings. Use a glue stick to attach them together, wrong sides facing. Stitch the perimeter of each.

3. For each back, stitch the long straight edges together, right sides facing. Turn each piece right side out, and iron it flat. Using a zigzag stitch, make a ½-inch (1.3 cm) casing for elastic as shown (figure 1).

4. Cut two pieces of elastic about 1 inch (2.5 cm) shorter than the length of the back pieces. Use a safety pin to thread the elastic through each casing. Pull the elastic a bit tight for a gathered effect, and pin each end flush with the ends of the casing. Stitch both ends of the back to secure the elastic.

5. With right sides facing, pin the ends of each back piece to a bootie top piece as shown in figure 2, and stitch the two together. Without opening or pressing this piece, lay the fleece top piece (lining) over it, right side facing down. Line it up with the outer fabric top piece on the bottom of the stack and stitch again across the seam you just made.

figure 1

figure 2

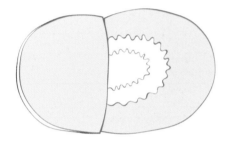

figure 3

6. Trim any excess fabric at the seams and open up the little sandwich of fabrics by turning the fleece lining piece around until it's under the outer top (figure 3). To secure the two layers together, run a decorative stitch across from side to side.

7. Pin the soles to the top oval shape, right sides together, with the sole on top. Stitch the perimeter as close to the edges as possible, with the sole on the bottom as you stitch to ensure a smoother, rounder bootie shape. Trim away any excess fabric, then turn the booties right side out.

cruisers

Baby will be kicking and screaming to get into these lightweight cruiser booties. The soles are made from durable canvas, and a drawstring top ensures the perfect fit. Tie them on and try to keep up.

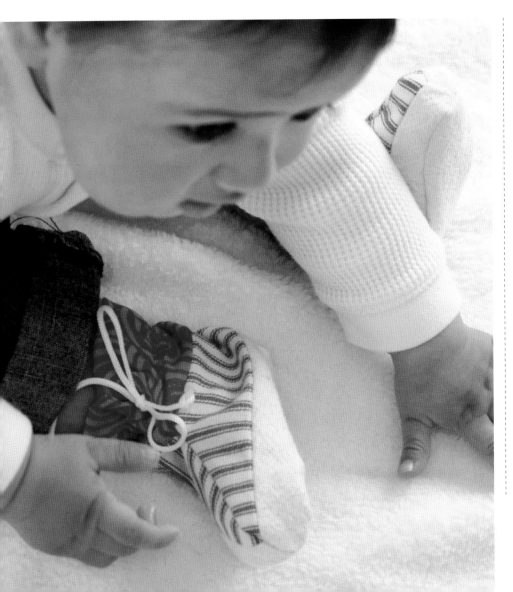

what you need

Sewing Kit (page 15)

¼ yard (22.9 cm) of cotton fabric

¼ yard (22.9 cm) of ticking

¼ yard (22.9 cm) of canvas

1 yard (91.4 m) of thin white cord

seam allowance

¼ inch (6 mm)

pattern pieces

top

sole

designer: **Joan K. Morris**

what you do

1. Cut fabric as follows:

- from the cotton, two 4½ x 14-inch (11.4 x 35.6 cm) strips

- from the ticking, two 1¾ x 14-inch (4.4 x 35.6 cm) strips

- from the canvas, two 1¼ x 14-inch (3.2 x 35.6 cm) strips

For each bootie, stitch three strips of fabric together, and press the seams open.

2. Using the pattern, cut out the bootie tops from the strips stitched in step 1 (figure 1). Cut two soles out of canvas.

3. For each bootie, fold the top edge of the cotton strip down to meet the first seam line, with the right sides of the fabric together. Using a ¼-inch (6 mm) seam allowance, begin to stitch the sides down; however, after stitching for ¾ inch (1.9 cm), leave ½ inch (1.3 cm) open on the seam for the casing, then continue stitching to the end. Turn right side out and push out the corners. Press.

4. For each bootie, run a stitch line across the cotton strip from the top of the opening to the other side top of the opening. Run another line of stitching ½ inch (1.3 cm) down from the first to create the casing. Run a piece of cord 18 inches (45.7 cm) long through the casing (figure 2).

5. Turn under and press the bottom edge of the cotton strip and hand stitch it in place. Fold the bootie in half, right sides together, matching the edges. Stitch from the bottom of the casing to the end of the toe stitch, using a ½-inch (1.3 cm) seam allowance. Clip the curves.

6. With the booties wrong side out, pin the tops to the soles and carefully stitch the perimeter of the sole. Clip the curves and turn right side out. Pull the cords, tie a bow, and turn the top edge over to make a little cuff.

Lace 'em up: These boots were made for...crawling.

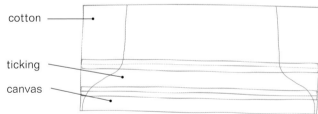

cotton

ticking

canvas

figure 1

figure 2

baby janes

Admit it: The apple of your eye will look like a peach in these mini Mary Janes. Wouldn't you like a pair, too?

what you need

Sewing Kit (page 15)

20-inch (50.8 cm) square of suede, leather, vinyl, or felt for the outer fabric

20-inch (50.8 cm) square of wool felt for the lining

Glue stick

2 matching medium-size buttons, preferably with a shank

seam allowance

⅛ inch (3 mm)

pattern pieces

top

sole

tab

designer: **Katherine Accettura**

what you do

1. Using the pattern, cut out all of the pieces—two of each from suede and two of each from felt—making sure to transfer the hash marks onto the sole pieces.

2. Lay the suede tabs on top of the felt tabs, wrong sides facing, and use a glue stick to attach them together. Stitch the perimeter of each.

3. Glue the tops and soles to their lining pieces, wrong sides facing. This will keep the pieces from slipping apart when you stitch them. Before the glue dries, slip the tab in between the suede and felt layers at the spot marked on the template. When dry, stitch the tabs in place. Also stitch the perimeters of both soles, and stitch around the U-shaped openings with a straight, zigzag, or decorative stitch (figure 1).

4. Fold the top pieces in half length-wise, right sides together, and stitch the back heel seam. Leave the top wrong side out and pin it to the sole pieces, right sides together. Line up the heel seam with the hash mark on the sole. Stitch around the oval shape with the sole portion up (figure 2).

5. Turn the shoes right side out. Securely sew on a button by hand, then slit a buttonhole in the tab. To avoid making it too big, cut it smaller than you think is needed, and gradually enlarge it enough to pull the button through.

figure 1

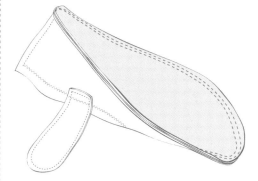

figure 2

moon booties

One small step for Mom; one giant leap for Baby! These purple moon booties are perfect for your little explorer. Whether crawling across the floor, cruising in a stroller, or swaying in a swing set, these boots are going places.

what you need

Sewing Kit (page 15)

¼ yard (22.9 cm) of lightweight vinyl

¼ yard (22.9 cm) of light corduroy

seam allowance

¼ inch (6 mm)

pattern pieces

top

sole

designer: **Joan K. Morris**

what you do

1. Using the pattern, cut two top pieces from the vinyl. Cut two top pieces and four sole pieces from the corduroy.

2. Place a vinyl top and a corduroy top right sides together. Machine stitch around the entire curved edge. Clip the curves (figure 1) and turn the top right side out. Press from the corduroy side. To keep the open edge along the bottom from slipping when stitched to the sole, machine baste the two pieces together as close to the edge as possible. Repeat with the other bootie top.

3. Fold a bootie top in half lengthwise with the corduroy inside. Machine stitch as close as possible to the edge, from the dot shown on the template to the end of the toe (figure 2). Repeat for the other bootie top.

4. Place two of the corduroy soles wrong sides together and machine baste the perimeter as close to the edge as possible. Repeat with the other two soles.

5. Turn the booties inside out and pin each sole in position. Machine stitch around the edge of each sole, and stitch again with a zigzag stitch to keep the edge from fraying. Trim any excess fabric and turn the booties right side out. Fold down the top edge of each to make cuffs.

Slip them on Baby, pop in some '80s tunes, and get ready to do the moonwalk.

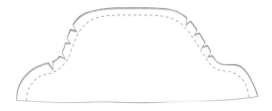

figure 1

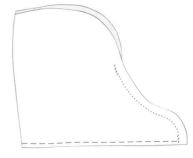

figure 2

bébé beret

Going downtown for a coffee? Your bundle of joy insists on wearing a hip *chapeau*. Slip this velvety black beret onto baby's head and say *bonjour* to traveling in style.

what you need

Sewing Kit (page 15)

¼ yard (22.9 cm) of velour fabric

¼ yard (22.9 cm) of cotton fabric for the lining

Small piece of hook-and-loop tape

seam allowance

½ inch (1.3 cm)

designer: **Wendi Gratz**

1. Cut out the following pieces:

- From both the velour and the lining, cut two 9-inch (22.9 cm) circles. To adjust for different sizes, see the box on page 48.

- On one velour and one lining circle cut above, cut a 4½-inch (11.4 cm) hole from the center. The finished piece should look like a ring that's 2½ inches (6.4 cm) wide all the way around (figure 1).

- From the velour, cut a 3 x 18-inch (7.6 x 45.7 cm) strip for the hatband, two 2 x 8½-inch (5.1 x 21.6 cm) rectangles for the chin straps, and a 2 x 3-inch (5.1 x 7.6 cm) rectangle for the nub at the top of the hat.

2. Stitch the short ends of the hatband together, right sides together, to make a continuous strip. Press the seam allowances open. Fold the strip in half lengthwise, wrong sides together, and press.

3. For each chin strap, turn one short end of the rectangle ¼ inch (6 mm) to the wrong side and press. Fold the rectangle in half lengthwise, wrong sides together, and press. Open the strap and fold both long edges to the center crease, refold along the crease, press, and topstitch (page 19). Set aside.

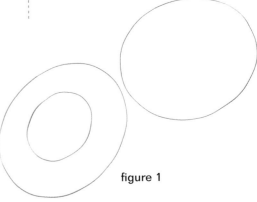

figure 1

4. To make the nub, fold the small rectangle in half, wrong sides together, to make a 1½ x 2-inch (3.8 x 5.1 cm) rectangle. Press, then fold it in half again to make a 1 x 1½-inch (2.5 x 3.8 cm) rectangle. Press, and open it back up. Fold the edges in to the center crease, as you did for the chin straps, and refold along the crease. The nub of fabric should now measure ½ x 1½ inches (1.3 x 3.8 cm). Topstitch all the way around the edges. Set aside.

5. Place the velour circle and velour ring right sides together. Stitch around the outside of the circle. Repeat with the lining pieces. Clip into the seam allowance all the way around the hat and the lining (page 20). Turn both right side out and press.

6. Fit the lining inside the hat, wrong sides together. Line up the raw edges of the insides of the rings. Pin the folded hat band around the hat opening, aligning the raw edges. Pin the chin straps to opposite sides of the hat (figure 2). Stitch all the way around the hat opening. (This single seam attaches the lining, hat, hatband, and chin straps.) Turn the seam allowance up into the hat and press.

7. Attach small squares of hook-and-loop tape to the ends of the chin straps (page 21).

8. Cut a tiny hole in the top of the hat. Slip the nub into the hole, leaving about 1 inch (2.5 cm) sticking out the top of the hat. Hand sew in place.

Et voilà, Baby's ready for an outing in *le parc*.

figure 2

ADJUSTING FOR HEAD SIZE

The measurements given are for a head that is 17 inches (43.2 cm) around. For a larger head, make the following adjustments:

- The diameter of the hole in the middle of the circle should be the circumference of the head, divided by 3.14, minus 1 inch (2.5 cm). Round up to the nearest ¼ inch (6 mm) for simplicity.
- The length of the hatband strip should be the circumference of the head plus 1 inch (2.5 cm).

no-knit hat

Want a warm winter hat for Baby, but don't know how to knit?
Simple. Turn a hand-me-down sweater into heads-up headwear!
All you need to do is sew and add embellishments. All Baby
needs to do is don it and look adorable.

what you need

Sewing Kit (page 15)

1 textured sweater

Felt scraps of varying colors

1 contrasting felted sweater (optional)

Three decorative snap heads and a snap setter

Leftover yarns of varying colors and textures

Scrap cardboard

seam allowance

½ inch (1.3 cm)

designer: **Joan K. Morris**

what you do

1. From the front of the textured sweater, cut an 11 x 22-inch (27.9 x 55.9 cm) rectangle, being sure to position the long side of the rectangle—which will become the bottom of the hat—along the bottom of the sweater. (If the bottom edge of the sweater isn't suitable, cut a slightly larger rectangle and turn a hem along the bottom using a zigzag stitch.)

2. Fold the sweater rectangle in half lengthwise, right sides facing, and stitch the ends together. Finger press the seam—you don't want to burn it with an iron—and use a zigzag stitch to tack down both sides (figure 1).

3. Copy the template on page 127 and cut three large flowers from scraps of felt or the felted sweater (to learn about felting, see the box on page 51). Pin them in place on the front of the hat, stretching and reshaping the petals as desired. Use a zigzag stitch around the edges to secure them to the hat.

figure 1

4. Using the template, cut out three smaller flowers from different colors of felt. Use a snap setter to attach a snap head in the center of each flower. Position each small flower onto a large one and use embroidery floss and a needle to hand stitch them in place, stitching through all layers.

5. To make the tassels, cut a 3 x 5-inch (7.6 x 12.7 cm) rectangle out of a scrap of cardboard. Wrap two different yarns around the 3-inch (7.6 cm) length of cardboard 10 times. Slip a separate piece of yarn under one side and tie it tightly around the pieces (figure 2). Slide the yarn off the cardboard and cut the opposite side. Wrap and tightly tie another piece of yarn around the tassel about ¾ inch (1.9 cm) down from the first tie. Trim any uneven ends. Make a second tassel.

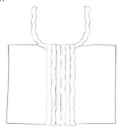

figure 2

6. Turn the hat inside out and place the tassels inside each corner with the tassel end inside and the yarn from the tied ends sticking out the raw edge. Pin across the top of the hat, marking a curve about 2 inches (5.1 cm) deep, evenly spaced across the top (figure 3). Stitch the edge and turn the hat right side out. Fluff the tassels.

When Baby wears this hat, make sure it's not too cold: it's so fun to play with it's not likely to stay on for long!

figure 3

FELTING A SWEATER

Felt has a wonderfully rich texture, is a sturdy fabric, and doesn't ravel. During felting, wool fibers tangle together and shrink. It's as easy as washing an old wool sweater in hot water with lots and lots of detergent and drying it on the hot setting in a dryer. Some sweaters might require more than one pass through the washing machine.

For best results, the sweater should be made of 100 percent lamb's wool, cashmere, or wool/angora blends. You can also try felting sweaters made from a wool blend with less than 10 percent acrylic or nylon fiber.

sprinkles sunhat

Oh, Baby! Everyone will want to know where you got this sweet little hat. With the yummy fabric and floppy brim, you'll be eating up the compliments *and* keeping out of the sun.

what you need

Sewing Kit (page 15)

½ yard (45.7 cm) of print fabric

¼ yard (22.9 cm) of muslin for the lining

⅔ yard (61 cm) of 1/2-inch (1.3 cm) single-fold bias tape

1½ inches (3.8 cm) of 5/8-inch (1.6 cm) hook-and-loop tape

seam allowance

¼ inch (6 mm)

pattern pieces

brim

wedge

designer: Rebeka Lambert

what you do

1. Using the pattern, cut out the following pieces:

- 6 wedges from the print fabric

- 6 wedges from the muslin lining

- 2 hat brims from the print fabric, cut on the fold

- two 2-inch-wide (5.1 cm) strips of the print fabric, one 10 inches (25.4 cm) long and the other 4½inches (11.4 cm) long

2. To make the crown of the hat, place two wedges of the print fabric right sides together and stitch along one edge. Keep adding the remaining wedges until a dome is created. Repeat with the muslin wedges to make the lining.

3. Fold each brim piece right sides together in a semicircle, and stitch the raw ends. Open them up to end up with two rings. Place the rings right sides together, matching up the seams, and stitch along the outer edge. Clip the curves (page 20), turn the brim right side out, and press. Topstitch along the outer edge of the brim.

4. With the hat and the lining wrong sides together, tuck the lining inside the hat, matching up the seams. Pin in place (figure 1).

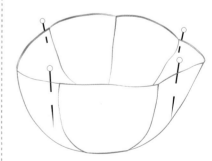

figure 1

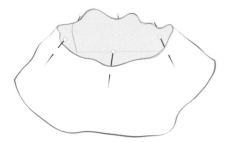

figure 2

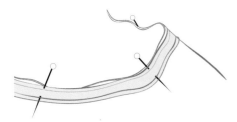

figure 3

5. Connect the brim to the crown of the hat by lining up the raw edges of the brim with the raw edges of the crown. Pin in place (figure 2), then baste to hold the layers together.

6. To hide the raw edges on the inside of the hat, bind it with bias tape. Open up a piece of the bias tape and line up the raw edge with the raw edges of the hat. Pin in place, then stitch in the fold all the way around the hat (figure 3). Turn the bias tape over the raw edges toward the inside of the hat and press. Stitch close to the edge of the outer fold, securing the bias tape to the hat.

7. Make straps for the hat, following the instructions on page 22. Cut ¾-inch (1.9 cm) strips of hook-and-loop tape, round the corners to avoid scratching Baby, and attach them to the ends of both straps (page 21).

8. Attach the straps to the hat by positioning one in line with the seam of the brim, matching up the end of the strap with the top of the bias tape. Stitch in place. Reinforce the strap by stitching again at the bottom of the bias tape where the dome and brim meet (figure 4). Repeat on the opposite side for the other strap, but check first that the hook-and-loop pieces line up properly.

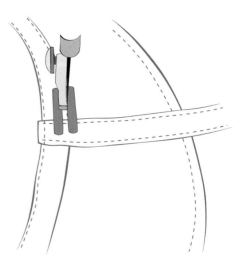

figure 4

yo-yo bow

Who's the smartest, most beautiful baby in the whole wide world? Why, yours, of course! So why not adorn that little noggin with a yo-yo bow? It's the crowning touch your little princess deserves.

what you need

Sewing Kit (page 15)

15 inches (38.1 cm) of ¾-inch (1.9 cm) elastic

⅛ yard (11.4 cm) of cotton floral fabric

Scraps of two other cotton floral fabrics

2 small buttons of slightly different size

seam allowance

½ inch (1.3 cm)

designer: **Joan K. Morris**

what you do

1. Measure the circumference of the baby's head and cut a piece of elastic of that length. Cut a strip of fabric one and a half times that length and 3 inches (7.6 cm) wide. Fold it right sides together lengthwise and stitch down the length and across one short end. Turn the strip right side out using a knitting needle or dry pen. Snip the short sewn edge, cutting off as little fabric as possible—just enough to remove the seam.

2. Use a safety pin to thread the elastic through the headband strip. Overlap the ends of the elastic and machine stitch them together. Pull the fabric ends together over the elastic and hand sew the opening closed.

3. Cut out three circles—one 2 inches (5.1 cm) in diameter, another 2¾ inches (7 cm) in diameter, and the last 3½ inches (8.9 cm) in diameter—each from a different fabric scrap. Make each into a yo-yo (page 25).

4. Stack all the yo-yos in order of size, with the largest on the bottom, the pucker side facing up on the bottom two, and the top yo-yo pucker side down. Hand sew all three together through the center, and then sew the buttons in place, with the smaller button on top. Make sure the buttons are very secure, so Baby can't chew them off and swallow them.

5. Position the yo-yos over the headband seam and hand sew them in place, hiding the stitches under the edge of each circle.

Baby, get ready for a flood of compliments when you're wearing this accessory.

elf caps

Too cute? No such thing. Some say elves inspired these caps while others cite gnomes. Either way, they're the perfect accessory for Mama's little helpers and will keep their heads nice and warm.

what you need

Sewing Kit (page 15)

½ yard (45.7 cm) of fleece for each hat

Decorative snap and snap setter (optional)

Yarn for a pom-pom (optional)

Scrap cardboard

seam allowance

½ inch (1.3 cm)

pattern pieces

blue cap: top
              earflaps

pink cap: top
              earflaps

designer: **Joan K. Morris**

MAKE THE BLUE CAP

what you do

1. Using the pattern, cut out two hat pieces and four earflap pieces from the fleece.

2. Pin the hat pieces right sides together. Stitch the sides, trim the seam allowances at the tip of the hat, and turn right side out. Push out the point with a knitting needle or chopstick. Tie a knot close to the point.

3. Pin two earflaps right sides together. Stitch both sides to the point, leaving the wide end open. Trim the point and turn the flaps right side out. Push out the point and tie a knot in the end close to the tip. Repeat to make the other earflap.

4. Use a zigzag stitch to close the wide ends of the earflaps. One at a time, center an earflap on a side seam of the hat as shown (figure 1), measuring up 1½ inches (3.8 cm) from the bottom raw edge. Stitch in place. Repeat with the other flap.

5. Turn the hat wrong side out. Fold up the bottom edge of the hat twice, so the earflaps hang from the bottom. Stitch the folded edge to the hat using a zigzag stitch (figure 2).

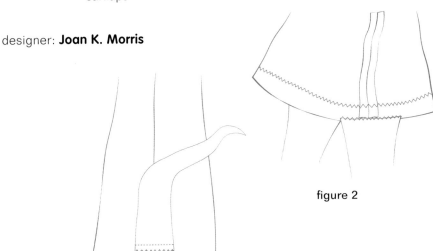

figure 1

figure 2

MAKE THE PINK CAP

what you do

1. Using the pattern, cut out two hat pieces and two earflap pieces from the fleece.

2. To make a pom-pom, cut a 2 x 5-inch (5.1 x 12.7 cm) piece of cardboard. Wrap yarn around the 2-inch (5.1 cm) side of the cardboard 20 times. Slip a separate 6-inch (15.2 cm) piece of yarn under one side and tie it tightly around the pieces (see page 26). Slide the yarn off the cardboard and cut the side opposite the tie. Make a second pom-pom and then tie the two together. Leave the 6-inch (15.2 cm) connecting yarns long, while fluffing out the shorter yarn and the ends evenly.

3. For this hat, the seam allowances will show on the outside of the hat. Pin the two hat pieces together with the wrong sides facing. At the tip, position the pom-pom with the connecting yarn ends tucked between the hat pieces. Stitch across the point to hold the pom-pom in place, and then stitch down each side. Trim the seam allowances to ⅛ inch (3 mm).

4. On each earflap, fold the wrong edges over ⅛ inch (3 mm). Stitch the sides and curved end, leaving the top straight edge alone.

5. Roll up the bottom edge of the hat about 1 inch (2.5 cm) with the wrong side facing out. Hand sew the top of the roll to the hat all the way around. Center the earflaps on the side seams and hand stitch in place.

6. Using the snap setter, set the snap in position on the bottom of the earflaps.

Isn't that pom-pom irresistible?

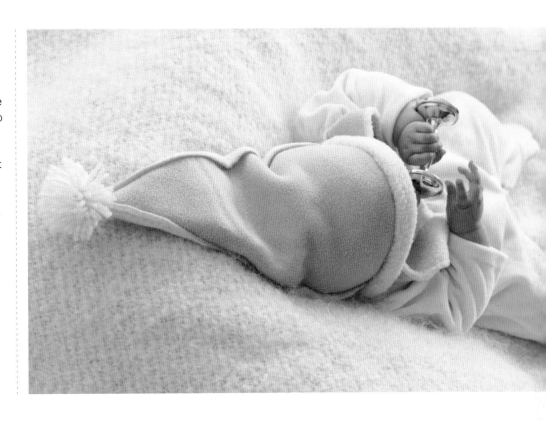

hold me cloche

This vintage-inspired hat is the perfect topper for the little one in your life. Not only is it utterly charming, but it's warm and reversible, too. Show Baby how to turn it inside and out, and watch her pick her favorite side.

what you need

Sewing Kit (page 15)

¼ yard (22.9 cm) of fabric A

¼ yard (22.9 cm) of fabric B

¼ yard (22.9 cm) of soft cotton batting

¼ yard (22.9 cm) of fabric C

2 pieces of ribbon

2 small buttons

seam allowance

⅜ inch (1 cm)

designer: **Tina Givens**

what you do

1. Enlarge the template on page 126. Fold fabric A in half and position the crown template piece with one side placed on the fold. Cut it out. Do the same for fabric B and the batting. For the rolled brim, cut a 20½ x 5-inch (52.1 x 12.7 cm) strip from fabric C and a 20½ x 2½-inch (52.1 x 6.4 cm) strip from either fabric A or B.

2. Lay the batting piece on the wrong side of the fabric A crown piece. Fold both layers with the fabric on the inside and the batting on the outside. Sew along the outer seams (figure 1). Open up the hat and line up the opposite, unstitched edges to form the hat top. Stitch along that edge (figure 2).

3. Repeat step 2 using fabric B—but omitting the batting—to make the lining of the hat.

4. Clip the curved seams (page 20) and turn the fabric A hat piece (the one with the batting) right side out. Finger press the seams. Leave the lining piece wrong side out and slide it inside the outer hat piece so you've got the wrong side of the hat against the wrong side of the lining. Baste the two together around the opening.

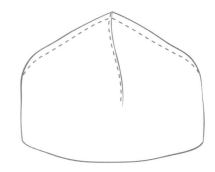

figure 1

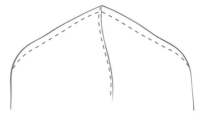

figure 2

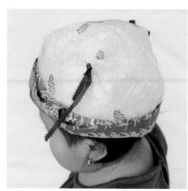
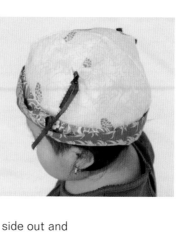

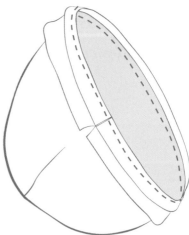

5. To make the brim, fold under the short ends of both strips by ½ inch (1.3 cm) and press. One at a time, fold each strip lengthwise, wrong sides together, and press. You should have two fabric strips, one narrower than the other, both with right sides facing out. Lay the two strips on top of one another, lining up the raw edges. Baste the raw edges together (figure 3).

6. Turn the hat wrong side out and attach the brim to the opening with the narrower strip on top. Start with one finished edge of it in the front center of the hat and pin it all around the hat edge until the end meets up at the starting point (figure 4). Stitch the brim in place.

7. Turn the hat right side out and press the seam allowance up away from the brim. Fold the narrower strip upward to encase the seam allowance, and hand sew in place.

8. To finish the hat, attach ribbons and buttons on any or all of the four corners. If using buttons, stitch them securely in place to prevent Baby from pulling them off and swallowing them.

Put it on Baby. Do you know what those gurgles mean? Baby wants a mirror.

figure 3

figure 4

prairie bonnet

Even urban babies want a little prairie flair now and then, and this bonnet's got cuteness covered. It would make even Laura Ingalls Wilder proud. For added charm, it ties with a wide satin ribbon.

what you need

Sewing Kit (page 15)

¼ yard (22.9 cm) of cotton fabric for the crown

5 x 20-inch (12.7 x 50.8 cm) strip of complementary cotton fabric for the brim

2 yards (1.8 m) of 1½-inch (3.8 cm) satin ribbon

1 yard (91.4 cm) of ⅛-inch (3 mm) white ribbon

seam allowance

½ inch (1.3 cm)

designer: **Joan K. Morris**

what you do

1. Enlarge the template on page 124. For the crown, cut two 7 x 15 ½-inch (17.8 x 39.4 cm) rectangles. From the complementary fabric, cut two brim pieces.

2. Stitch each brim piece to a crown piece lengthwise, right sides facing. Press the seams toward the crown. Place these two pieces right sides together and stitch around the sides and curved end (figure 1). Clip the curves (page 20), trim the seam allowance, and turn right side out.

3. To make the casing for the ribbon in the back of the bonnet, fold over both fabrics on the long raw edge of the bonnet ¼ inch (6 mm) and press. Fold over again ½ inch (1.3 cm) and pin or press. Stitch the length of the folded edge.

4. Fold the bonnet in half (as it will be worn) and find the top center of the hat. Place a pin on the center point at the seam between the brim and crown. Fold the wider satin ribbon in half lengthwise and mark its center. Match up these center points as you place the wrong side of the ribbon on the right side of the hat. Pin the ribbon in place on the crown, along the seamline at the brim. Stitch as close as possible to the edges of the ribbon: down the length, across at the side of the hat, down the opposite length, and across the other side of the hat to the starting point. Trim the ends of the large satin ribbon on the diagonal.

5. Use a safety pin to thread the narrow ribbon through the casing (figure 2). Remove the pin and pull both ends of the ribbon to tie a bow.

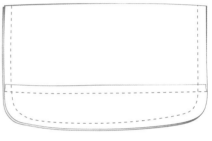

figure 1

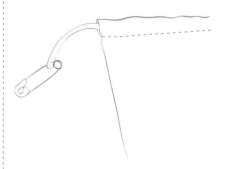

figure 2

on the town

Brooks Brothers has got nothing on you, Baby. Pair pinstripes with a tie for the gentlemen, or appliqué a set of satin beads for the ladies. You're never too young to play dress up!

what you need

Sewing Kit (page 15)

8-inch (20.3 cm) square of paper-backed fusible web

Scrap fabric for the appliqués

¼ yard (22.9 cm) of fabric for the bib

Small piece of hook-and-loop tape

seam allowance

¼ inch (6 mm)

designer: **Wendi Gratz**

what you do

1. Enlarge the templates on pages 122–123 and trace the appliqué of your choice—necktie or necklace—onto the paper side of the fusible adhesive. Cut the piece(s) out, leaving about 1 inch (2.5 cm) around the edges of the tracing. Following the manufacturer's instructions, fuse the adhesive to the wrong side of the scrap fabric. Cut out the appliqué shape(s).

2. Cut two pieces of fabric for the bib front and back. Fuse the appliqué to the right side of the bib front, allowing for the seam along the top. Satin stitch (page 28) around the appliqué piece(s); for the tie, this includes stitching the bottom of the "knot," shown as a dotted line on the template.

3. Pin the bib front and back together, right sides facing, and stitch the outer edge. Leave a 2- to 3-inch (5.1 to 7.6 cm) opening on one side. Clip and notch the seam allowance at all curves, especially the tight ones around the neck (page 20). Turn the bib right side out through the opening in the side. Press the bib flat and topstitch all the way around the edge.

4. Stitch one square of hook-and-loop tape to each side of the bib, one square to the front, and the other to the back (page 21).

Now let's practice for the future: *Garçon*, what's tonight's special?

plushy pocket

Vroom! Open up, Baby, the spoon plane is coming! For pilots who could use some work on their aim, this bib boasts pockets and absorbent fabrics to catch any spills. Fasten your seat belt, Baby, it's going to be a yummy ride.

what you need

Sewing Kit (page 15)

¼ yard (22.9 cm) of textured fabric

1 hand towel

18 inches (45.7 cm) of ⅝-inch (1.6 cm) decorative grosgrain ribbon

1 yard (91.4 cm) of ¾-inch (1.9 cm) grosgrain ribbon for the ties

seam allowance

½ inch (1.3 cm)

designer: Joan K. Morris

what you do

1. Enlarge the template on page 127 and cut the bib front from the textured fabric. From the finished edge of the hand towel, cut a 3¼x 8-inch (8.3 x 20.3 cm) strip for the pocket, then cut out the bib back any place on the towel.

2. Cut an 8-inch (20.3 cm) piece from the ⅝-inch (1.6 cm) grosgrain. Also cut two 3¼-inch (8.3 cm) pieces. Mark the pocket in equal thirds and pin the short pieces of ribbon on the dividing lines. Stitch one edge of each ribbon. Pin the longer piece of ribbon along the top edge of the pocket strip, covering the top edges of both short pieces (figure 1). Stitch both edges of the long ribbon.

3. Pin the pocket strip to the bottom edge of the bib front. Baste around the sides and bottom edge of the pocket strip. Through both layers of fabric, stitch the unsewn edges of the two short ribbon pieces. This will create three pockets.

4. Cut two 18-inch (45.7 cm) pieces from the ¾-inch (1.9 cm) grosgrain. Pin one end of each ribbon to the front bib shoulders (figure 2). Machine baste the ribbons in place.

5. Pin the front and the back of the bib right sides together, making sure the ribbon is tucked inside and not caught in any seams. Stitch around the edge, leaving 5 inches (12.7 cm) open at the bottom. Clip the corners and curves (page 20) and turn the bib right side out through the opening. Press the bib flat, folding the open edges in. Hand sew the opening closed. Topstitch along the top of the bib.

Hey, Baby, look what's in the pocket!

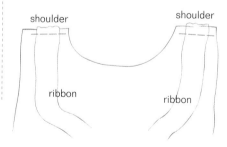

pin long ribbon on top

one line of stitching

figure 1

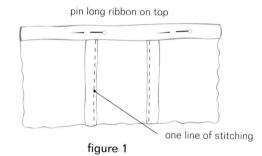

shoulder   shoulder

ribbon   ribbon

figure 2

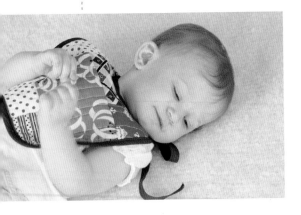

quilted bib

Quilts aren't just for sleepy time anymore. This quilted bib has got Baby covered from breakfast through midnight snacks—and everything in between. Soft cotton flannel backs the bib, and cotton batting in between will keep Baby's clothes spotless.

what you need

Sewing Kit (page 15)

8 pieces of coordinating scrap material

11 x 14-inch (27.9 x 35.6 cm) piece of cotton batting

11 x 14-inch (27.9 x 35.6 cm) piece of cotton flannel for the backing

1 package of ½-inch (1.3 cm) double-fold bias tape in a contrasting color

seam allowance

¼ inch (6 mm)

designer: Jessie Senese

what you do

1. Cut rectangles of the scraps and stitch them together to create a piece of patchwork 11 x 14 inches (27.9 x 35.6 cm). Any number of designs are possible; the illustration on page 73 shows how this one was put together (figure 1). Press the finished piece flat and lay it right side up on top of the batting. Pin the two together.

2. Quilt the material by lining up one raw edge with the machine's presser foot and sewing a straight line. When you reach the bottom edge, lift the presser foot with the needle still in position and turn the fabric 90°. Stitch the width you desire, turn the fabric again, and stitch a line parallel to the first (figure 2). Repeat this process until you've quilted the entire piece. Press, if needed.

3. Enlarge the template on page 121. Place the flannel backing piece right side down, and lay the quilted piece right side up on top of it. Pin the two pieces together. Place the bib template on top of the quilted piece, then use a water-soluble marker to trace its outline. Starting on one of the long sides, stitch along the marked line all the way around the bib.

4. Carefully cut ⅛ inch (3 mm) outside the seam line, making sure not to confuse the sewn seam with the quilting lines. Using one continuous strip, encase the perimeter of the bib in double-fold bias tape, being sure to place the narrower width on the right (top) side (page 27) and taking extra care at the corners (figure 3). Stitch the entire length of the bias tape about ⅛ inch (3 mm) from the edge. Trim the tails of the bias tape to line up with the neckline of the bib.

(continues on page 74)

figure 1

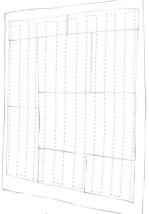

figure 2

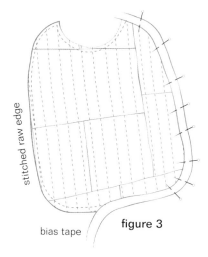

stitched raw edge

bias tape

figure 3

5. Cut a strip of bias tape about 31 inches (78.7 cm) total—long enough to go around a baby's neck and tie in a bow. Trim the ends. Find the center of the bias tape and pin it to the center of the bib front's neckline. Encase the neckline by pinning the bias tape along it. Stitch along the length of the tape, ⅛ inch (3 mm) from its edge, closing it and binding the entire neckline in one seam.

patchwork set

This bib and burp cloth set would make a trendy present to new parents, and with all that pretty ribbon, Baby will look like the sweetest gift of all. Coordinate an assortment of colorful ribbon and rickrack to create your own unique patchwork.

what you need

Sewing Kit (page 15)

½ yard (45.7 cm) of muslin

½ yard (45.7 cm) of terry cloth

16-inch (40.6 cm) square of paper-backed fusible web

Assortment of ribbons and trims in various widths and colors

Bronze snap and snap setter

seam allowance

¼ inch (6 mm)

designer: Rebeka Lambert

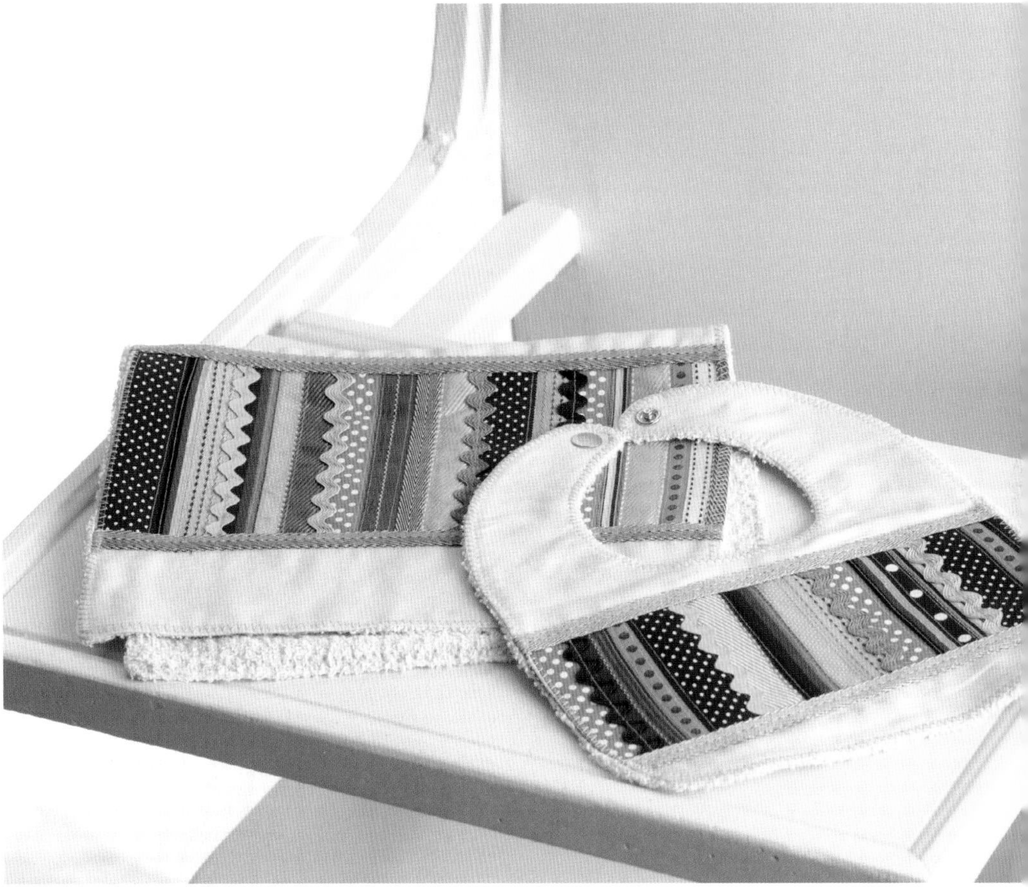

what you do

1. Enlarge the template on page 124. Cut the bib front from the muslin and the back from the terry cloth. For the burp cloth, cut an 11 x 18-inch (27.9 x 45.7 cm) rectangle from both the muslin and the terry cloth. Also cut two pieces of fusible web: one that's 9½ x 3½ inches (24.1 x 8.9 cm) for the bib; the other, 11 x 5 inches (27.9 x 12.7 cm) for the burp cloth.

2. For the bib, cut ribbon pieces that are 3½ inches (8.9 cm) long. For the burp cloth, cut pieces 5 inches (12.7 cm) long. In both cases, cut enough to cover the fusible web, and arrange the ribbons as you wish.

3. With the iron set no higher than for wool, carefully adhere each piece of ribbon to the fusible backings. Be sure to butt the edges of the ribbons and don't let the iron touch the adhesive. After all the pieces have been attached, let the adhesive cool before carefully removing the paper backing.

4. Position the ribbon patches on the right side of the muslin for both the bib and the burp cloth. For the bib, position the patch 1½ inches (3.8 cm) from the bottom edge; for the burp cloth, 3 inches (7.6 cm) from the edge. With your iron, carefully adhere the ribbon to the muslin. Be careful not to melt the ribbon; it helps to flip the muslin over to iron on the back side. Trim any excess ribbon that may be hanging over the edge.

5. Stitch the ribbon to the muslin to secure it, stitching down each length of ribbon and back up again on the other side. For added interest, stitch a few lengths of rickrack on top of the ribbons (one line of stitching down the middle will suffice). Finish by stitching a length of ribbon across the raw edges of the ribbon at both the top and the bottom of the ribbon patch.

6. Pin the terry cloth to the front of the bib, right sides facing. Stitch around the perimeter, leaving a 3- to 4-inch (7.6 to 10.2 cm) opening on one side for turning. Do the same for the burp cloth. Clip and notch the seam allowance at all curves, especially the tight ones around the neck (page 20).

7. Turn both the bib and the burp cloth right sides out, smoothing out the edges. For both, turn the raw edges of the opening to the inside and pin it closed. Topstitch near the edge all the way around, which closes up the opening and adds a nice finish.

8. On the bib, attach a snap to the neck straps using the snap setter of your choice.

Don't be surprised if Baby wants to enhance the look of the pretty ribbons with his own artfully smeared additions!

bunny baby

Hop to it! This bib features a fabric with graphics your little honey-bunny will love. Why not make one for every day of the week?

what you need

Sewing Kit (page 15)

¼ yard (22.9 cm) of cotton fabric for the front

¼ yard (22.9 cm) of contrasting cotton fabric for the back

Small piece of hook-and-loop tape

seam allowance

¼ inch (6 mm)

designer: Wendi Gratz

what you do

1. Enlarge the template on page 122; cut a bib front from the cotton fabric and a bib back from the contrasting fabric. With right sides facing, stitch the front and back together, leaving a 2- to 3-inch (5.1 to 7.6 cm) opening on one side. Clip and notch the seam allowance at all curves, especially the tight ones around the neck (page 20).

2. Turn the bib right side out through the opening in the side. Press the bib flat and topstitch all the way around the outer edge.

3. Cut a small square of hook-and-loop tape. Stitch one square to each side of the bib. Be careful to stitch one square to the front, and the other to the back (page 21).

Tie it on Baby, and do the bunny-hop.

VARIATION

If you want a padded bib, no problem. Use the template to cut a third bib shape from a flat sheet of batting. In step 1, place it on top of the unstitched bib pieces, and stitch it along with the rest. When you turn the bib right side out, the padding will tuck inside.

birdie rattles

Curious babies, rejoice! These soft, squishy rattles are just for you. These tweet creatures rattle in a most fascinating manner, and the beaks, wings, and tails are just the thing for pulling and chewing. Conveniently, the tie handles can also attach to strollers, high chairs, or play gyms.

what you need

Sewing Kit (page 15)

¼ yard (22.9 cm) of washable velour or other fabric for the body and wings

Fabric scraps for the beak and tail

Small bells or 5 beads

Pill bottle or other small, lidded plastic container

Polyester fiberfill

Yarn scraps for the eyes

seam allowance

⅛ inch (3 mm)

pattern pieces

body

wing

beak

tail

designer: **Suzie Fry**

what you do

1. Cut out the pattern pieces and lay them on the fabric. Cut two body pieces, four wing pieces, two beak pieces, and one tail piece from the corresponding fabrics. (You can fit one set of wings in the cutout between the handles on the body.) **Note:** Because knit fabrics usually stretch more in one direction than the other, pay particular attention to the grain of the fabric and make sure that the maximum stretch goes across the bird body (from side to side). Some knits, such as velour, may also have a nap or pile, which sits flatter in one direction than the other, so orient all of the pieces in the same direction.

2. Snip the tail piece as marked to form a fringe. Roll the base of the tail and stitch the edge closed.

3. Pin the beak pieces with right sides together and sew along the two sides. Clip the seam allowance (page 20) at the beak point and turn the beak right side out. Stitch a line through the center of the beak from the tip to the base.

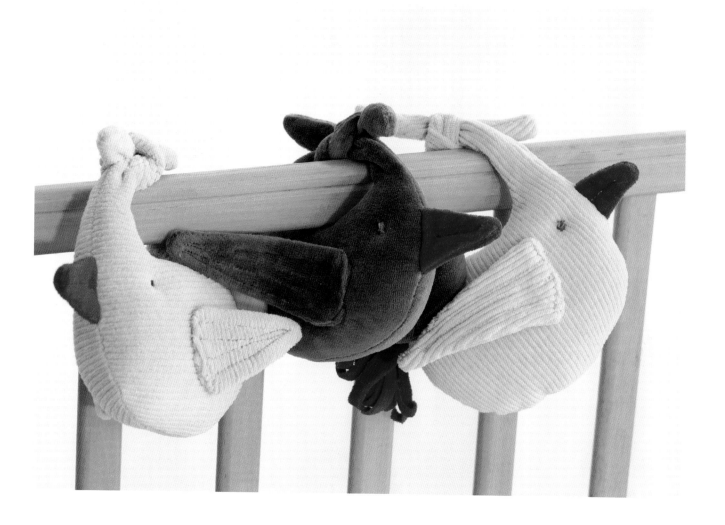

4. For each wing, put two wing pieces right sides together and stitch around the edge, leaving an opening at the wide end. Trim the seam allowances and turn the wing right side out. Tuck in the seam allowance at the opening and stitch the end. Stitch some lines along the wings, starting at the wide end and converging at the tip.

5. On the right side of the body pieces, pin the wings in place. Make sure they both face the right way: when lying side by side they should be mirror images of each other. Stitch in place along the wide end of each wing. Place the tail and beak facing in on the sides as shown (figure 1). Pin the layers together, and stitch around the edge of the body pieces, leaving an opening on the inside curve between the handles. Trim the ends, clip the curves, and turn the rattle right side out.

6. To make a rattle insert, place the bells or beads inside the plastic container and close it. (As an alternative, you can use caged bells sold for cat toys as a rattle insert, or take apart a cheap rattling toy.) Use fabric scraps to cover the rattle insert, securing it with a few rough stitches. This makes the surface of the insert less slippery and helps prevent it from working out of the center of the toy. Set aside.

7. Stuff the rattle with fiberfill, concentrating on the ends and the base of the body. You don't need to stuff the handles. When the body is about two-thirds full, place the rattle insert firmly in the center. Add more stuffing until the toy is firm. Hand sew the opening closed. Tie a double knot in the handles.

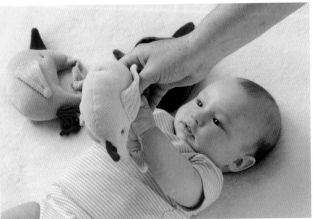

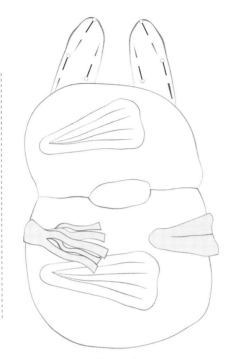

8. Thread the scrap yarn onto a large needle. Push the needle through the head at the marked eye position, all the way through to the eye position on the other side. Take the needle back through to the first side, but leave extra yarn dangling on both sides. Remove the needle and securely knot the two ends of yarn, pulling a little to pinch the toy in. Trim the ends.

Baby, are you ready to shake, rattle, and roll?

figure 1

oh, kimono

Playing dress-up games set in ancient Arabia or the Orient of yore? Need a cover-up for a pool party? This robe is oh-so-perfect. The design is stylish and roomy, and it ties together simply with a single bow. Baby will always say *yes* to this kimo-*no*.

what you need

Sewing Kit (page 15)

½ yard (45.7 cm) of fabric

1 package of ½-inch (1.3 cm) double-fold bias tape

1 button

3⅛ inches (8 cm) of elastic

seam allowance

¼ inch (6 mm)

pattern pieces

front

back

sleeve

designer: **Rebeka Lambert**

what you do

1. Lay out the pattern pieces along the grain of the fabric, and cut them out.

2. With right sides together, stitch the kimono front to the kimono back at the shoulder seams.

3. Fold each sleeve in half lengthwise to find and mark the shoulder center. With the right sides together, pin each sleeve to the kimono, lining up the center of the sleeve with the shoulder seam (figure 1). Stitch, trim the seams, and press.

4. With right sides together, stitch the sides of the kimono from each sleeve cuff to the bottom edge. Clip the underarm curves, turn right side out, and press the seams.

5. Using one continuous strip, pin double-fold bias tape to encase the side and neck edges of the kimono, being sure to place the narrower width on the right side (page 22). Topstitch close to the outside folded edge. Do the same around the ends of the sleeves.

6. Hem the bottom of the kimono with a narrow double-folded hem (page 20).

7. From the remainder of the bias tape, cut two ties, each 12 inches (30.5 cm) long. Tuck in the ends and stitch along all open sides to enclose the raw edges. Pin one tie in place on the outside front corner of the kimono and line up the other tie under the armhole seam. Check that, when tied, they'll secure the front of the kimono. Stitch them in place.

8. Open the kimono. To secure the inside flap, sew a button on its corner and stitch a loop of elastic about ¾ inch (1.9 cm) down from the armhole on the underarm seam. The loop wraps around the button to close the robe (figure 2).

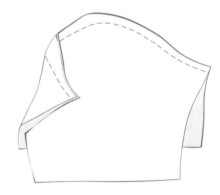

figure 1

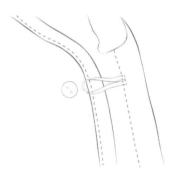

figure 2

under cover

No need to get bummed over drab, boring diapers. Hide them under a snazzy cover-up. Baby will be glad you did.

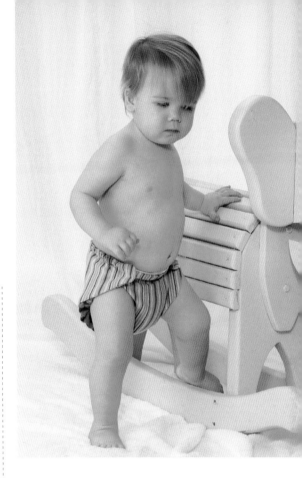

what you need

Sewing Kit (page 15)

⅝ yard (57.2 cm) of striped stretch knit

¼ yard (22.9 cm) of complementary stretch knit

1 package of ¼-inch (6 mm) elastic

6 inches (15.2 cm) of ¾-inch (1.9 cm) iron-on hook-and-loop tape

Ballpoint needle for your sewing machine

seam allowance

⅝ inch (1.6 cm)

designer: **Valerie Shrader**

what you do

1. Enlarge the appropriate template on pages 128–129. Cut two diaper covers from the striped stretch knit and two gussets from the complementary stretch knit. Transfer all markings except for the fastener boxes.

2. Using a ballpoint needle in your sewing machine, make a line of basting stitches ½ inch (1.3 cm) away from the outer, longer edge of each gusset. Turn under ½ inch (1.3 cm) to make a casing for the elastic, easing as you fold. Stitch close to the edge. (Because it's knit fabric, you don't need to turn under the raw edge.)

3. Wrap the elastic around your baby's chubby little thigh to find a comfortable fit, and cut two pieces to that length. Insert one into each casing and adjust the gathers evenly. Stitch each end of the elastic in place to secure (figure 1).

4. With right sides facing and markings matched, baste the gusset in place. Stretch the gusset to fit, if necessary.

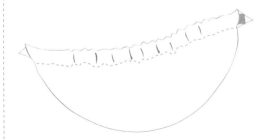

figure 1

5. Using the remaining cover as the lining, stitch the cover and lining together with right sides facing, making sure the gussets are between the layers. Leave the back open between the marked dots. Trim the corners and clip the curves (page 20). Turn inside out through the opening.

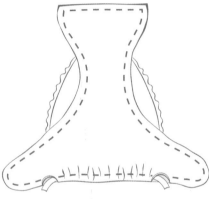

figure 2

6. Make a casing along the opening by folding in the raw edges toward one another. Stitch ⅛ inch (3 mm) from the opening and again ½ inch (1.3 cm) from the opening, leaving 1 inch (2.5 cm) open at each marked dot to insert the elastic (figure 2). Cut a piece of elastic 10 ¼ inches (26 cm) long. Thread it through the entire casing and stitch in place at both ends. Stitch across the open edges of the casing, stretching the cover as you stitch.

7. Position the hook-and-loop tape to the diaper cover front and back as indicated on the template and apply according to the manufacturer's instructions. If you don't mind the stitching showing on the right side, stitch around the perimeter of the tape to keep it down securely.

ring around

Baby, have I got a mission for you! Grab these brightly colored fabric rings and put them on the post, then pull them back off. It's a valuable lesson in hand-eye coordination, but really, who cares about that? Just have fun.

what you need

Sewing Kit (page 15)

5-inch (12.7 cm) wooden disk (precut from a craft store)

¾ x 8-inch (1.9 x 20.3 cm) wooden dowel

1½-inch (3.8 cm) flat-head wood screw

Wood glue

1¼-inch (3.2 cm) wooden ball

1½-inch (3.8 cm) dowel screw (both ends should be pointed)

Craft paint and paintbrush

Clear nontoxic sealer

Assorted cotton scraps of 6 to 8 different fabrics (for the larger ring they need to be at least 8 inches [20.3 cm] square)

6 assorted ribbons, ½ to 1½ inches (1.3 to 3.8 cm) wide

Polyester fiberfill

Drill and drill bits

Pliers

seam allowance

½ inch (1.3 cm)

designer: **Joan K. Morris**

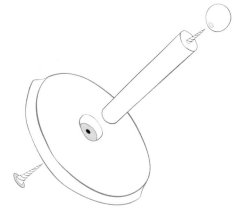

figure 1

what you do
MAKE THE WOODEN STRUCTURE

1. Locate the center top of the wooden disk. With a ¾-inch (1.9 cm) bit, drill a hole about halfway through the disk, achieving just enough depth to push the dowel into it. With a small bit to match the wood screw diameter, drill a hole the rest of the way through the disk. Dab a little wood glue into the larger hole and place the dowel in the hole. From the bottom, screw in the wood screw through the bottom and into the dowel.

2. At the top center of the dowel, use the small bit to drill a hole about ¾ inches (1.9 cm) deep. Drill a second hole of the same depth in the wooden ball. Use pliers to screw one end of the dowel screw into the hole. Screw the ball onto the top until the dowel and the ball meet.

3. Paint the wood your color of choice. Allow to dry, then paint with a few coats of nontoxic clear sealer.

MAKE THE RINGS

1. Enlarge the template on page 126 and cut the circles out of the cotton scraps. Cut two circles of fabric of each size to serve as the top and bottom of each ring.

2. Add ribbon and other decoration to some of the rings. (Some options are explained below.) To make the un-embellished rings, pin a pair of circles right sides together and stitch all the way around the edge. Don't turn *any* of the rings right side out—that comes later.

- To make a ribbon ruffle, measure the outer edge of a ring, double that measurement, and cut that length from 1½-inch (3.8 cm) ribbon. If the ribbon has a wire edge, gather the edge on one side by pulling the wire. If there's no wire, baste along one edge and gather by pulling the thread (page 26). Pin the gathered edge of the ribbon to the edge of a circle as shown

(figure 2). Baste the ribbon in place. Where the ends meet, fold and stitch them together. Place the other circle of the same size right sides together over the ribbon and pin. Stitch all the way around the edge.

- To make a ring with folded ribbon tabs, cut 2-inch (5.1 cm) pieces of ½-inch (1.3 cm) ribbon and fold them in half, right sides facing out. Pin the folded pieces to the right side of the fabric as shown, spaced evenly around the circle (figure 3). Machine baste them in place, then stitch a second circle on top as described above.

3. To make the center hole, mark the center of each ring with a dot. Draw a 1¼-inch (3.2 cm) circle in the center of the ring, and stitch along its entire circumference. Cut through the seams from the edge of the ring straight to the center as shown (figure 4). On the pieces with ribbon edging, be sure to cut between the stitched ends of the ruffle or between folded tabs. To keep the seams from opening, add reinforcing hand stitching ¼ inch (6 mm) in from each cut.

4. Turn the rings right side out by running one end through the other. Line up the cut edges on one side of the ring and hand sew them together from seam to seam, leaving the other side open. Stuff fiberfill through the opening in both directions until the whole ring is tightly stuffed. Pull the ends of the fabric together and hand sew them closed.

5. Add further embellishments as desired; some options are listed below.

- To secure scrunched-up ribbon on the edge of a ring, cut a 1-inch (2.5 cm) ribbon twice the circumference of the ring. Baste down the middle of the ribbon lengthwise and gather it. Pin it around the edge of the ring, lining up the basting seam with the outer seam of the ring. Hand sew it in place securely.

- For a wavy ribbon effect, cut a piece of ½-inch (1.3 cm) ribbon one and a half times as long as the circumference of the ring. Hand sew the ribbon along the seam of the ring by scrunching it and tacking it securely every ½ inch (1.3 cm) or so.

- Weave a decorative ribbon around the folded tabs of a circle and hand sew it in place.

6. Place the rings on the pole. The holes may initially seem tight, but they'll stretch.

figure 2

figure 3

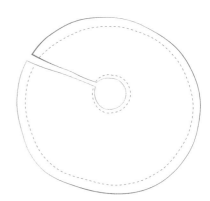

figure 4

yo-yo mobile

It's a bird, it's a plane, it's a yo-yo mobile! Pick bold colors and fabrics to match your nursery theme and hang the mobile over the crib or changing table. Baby will be endlessly entertained.

what you need

Sewing Kit (page 15)

⅛ yard (11.4 cm) of 5 different cotton fabrics

Inner hoop of an 8-inch (20.3 cm) embroidery hoop

2½ yards (2.3 m) of ¾-inch (1.9 cm) satin ribbon

5 yards (4.6 m) of ¼-inch (6 mm) satin ribbon

Hot glue gun

designer: **Belinda Andresson**

what you do

1. To create the yo-yos, make a template of a 4-inch (10.2 cm) circle, trace it onto the fabrics 48 times, and cut each one out. Make the yo-yos as described on page 25.

2. Randomly divide the yo-yos into six groups of eight. Hand sew each group of eight together on opposite sides to form a chain.

3. To attach each finished chain to the embroidery hoop, pass a needle and thread through the edge of a yo-yo at the end of the chain, wrap the thread around the hoop, and pass it back through the yo-yo. Do this a few times until the chain is secure, and then tie a knot. Be sure to evenly space the chains of yoyos around the hoop.

4. Cut four 24-inch (61 cm) strips of the wider ribbon. Evenly space the four ribbons around the hoop, and secure each one with a knot. Secure the short end of the knot to the inside of the hoop with some hot glue.

5. Secure one end of the narrow ribbon to the inside of the hoop with hot glue, and then wind the ribbon tightly around the entire hoop (figure 1), covering the thread and base of the ribbon ties as you go. When you reach the end, place a large dollop of hot glue on the inside of the hoop and secure the end of the ribbon to the hoop.

6. Gather the wide ribbon ties about 14 inches (35.6 cm) away from the hoop and fold them over to create a 6-inch (15.2 cm) loop. Stitch across the ribbons and backstitch several times to secure the loop (figure 2). Trim off any excess ribbon. Use the leftover wide ribbon to make a bow over the stitching, to cover it.

Hang up the mobile. What do you think, Baby—better than TV, huh?

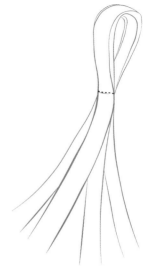

figure 1

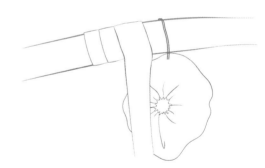

figure 2

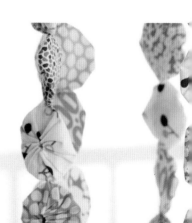

beautiful bloomers

Plain white diapers—how dull. Pooh-pooh the notion! Baby wants some sass, and she's got it with these cheeky bloomers. With layer upon layer of ruffles, she'll be sitting pretty.

what you need

Sewing Kit (page 15)

½ yard (45.7 cm) of printed stretch knit for the bloomers

¼ yard (22.9 cm) of complementary stretch knit for the leg panels and ruffles

1 package of ¼-inch (6 mm) elastic

Ballpoint needle for your sewing machine

Serger (optional)

seam allowance

⅝ inch (1.6 cm) unless otherwise noted

pattern pieces

front

back

leg panel

designer: **Valerie Shrader**

what you do

1. Cut out the following pattern pieces:

- from the printed knit, 2 bloomer pieces. Transfer all markings.

- from the complementary knit, 2 leg panels. Transfer all markings.

- from the complementary knit, four 2 x 24-inch (5.1 x 61 cm) pieces for the ruffles

2. Using a ballpoint needle in your sewing machine, stitch the leg panels to the bloomers with a ¼-inch (6 mm) seam. Press the seam open.

3. Use the serger to make a rolled hem on each bloomer leg. (If you don't own a serger, hem the legs as desired.)

4. Wrap the elastic around your baby's plump little thigh to find a comfortable fit, and cut two pieces of that length. Place one on a leg panel along the marked line. Stitch in place down the center of the elastic, stretching it to fit as you stitch. Repeat for the other leg (figure 1).

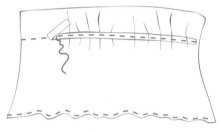

figure 1

figure 2

5. Stitch the front center seam, and then stitch the back center seam. Stitch again to reinforce the seams. Trim each seam and clip the curves (page 20).

6. Finish all raw edges of each ruffle with a rolled hem, using the serger. (If you don't have a serger, finish the edges as desired.) Baste a row of gathering stitches along one side of each ruffle about ¼ inch (6 mm) from the edge and gather each ruffle to fit the length indicated on the pattern piece (page 26). Beginning with the bottom ruffle, pin and stitch each ruffle in place, matching the basted stitch line to the marked stitch line from the pattern (figure 2).

7. Use the serger to finish the raw edge at the waist with a basic overlock stitch. (If you don't have a serger, finish the edge as desired.) Make a casing for the elastic by folding under at the waist as indicated on the template. Pin and stitch along the bottom edge, leaving an opening at the back to insert the elastic. Wrap the elastic around your baby's cute little potbelly to find a comfortable fit, and cut it. Feed it through the casing, and stitch the ends together. Stitch the opening closed.

8. With right sides together, stitch the crotch seam, and then stitch it again for reinforcement. Clip the curves, trim the seam, and turn the bloomers right side out.

soft blocks

What are the building blocks for baby fun? Something safe, something soft, and something colorful! And these blocks have it all. Choose bright fabrics and prints that Baby will find irresistible.

what you need

Sewing Kit (page 15)

4 coordinating scraps of fabric per block

Chenille fabric scraps

Polyester or cotton fiberfill

seam allowance

¼ inch (6 mm)

designer: **Jessie Senese**

what you do

1. Using a rotary cutter, ruler, and cutting mat (page 15), cut four 4-inch (10.2 cm) squares from cotton fabrics, and two 4-inch (10.2 cm) squares from chenille fabric. Lay out the fabrics in the pattern shown, with the chenille at D and F (figure 1).

2. With right sides together, stitch square B to square D; then D to E; then E to F. Stitch blocks A and C last, on either side of D. Press the squares flat and lay them right side up. Turn the top edge of the B block under ¼ inch (6 mm) and press. Do the same for the bottom edge of the F block. These two blocks will be stitched together later, and pressing them now will make that step easier.

3. With the right side facing up, position the D square on the bottom and turn up the surrounding squares. Pin the sides, right sides together (figure 2). Stitch the sides together, stopping and starting ¼ inch (6 mm) from each end. Line up the top of B with the bottom of F, but leave this section unstitched. Make sure that all eight corners meet.

4. Turn the block right side out through the opening, using a pencil or chopstick to push out the corners. Stuff the block with fiberfill.

5. Line up the pressed seams of the B and F blocks and hand sew the opening. Bury the thread tails inside the block.

Do you think Baby's ready to learn to juggle?

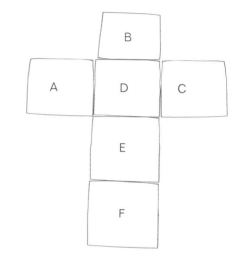

figure 1

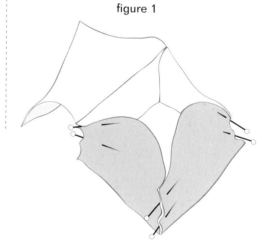

figure 2

too-too fun

A tutu, slipper, and bib set. Not only will your little girl look charming and talented, but she'll also feel like a real ballerina. For boys, you can skip the no-sew tutu and choose masculine colors for the patchwork bib and slippers. Either way, the look is *en pointe*.

MAKE THE TUTU

what you need

Sewing Kit (page 15)

20 inches (50.8 cm) of ¾-inch (1.9 cm) elastic

4 yards (3.7 m) of tulle

60 inches (152.4 cm) of 4-inch (10.2 cm) satin ribbon for the sash (optional)

22-inch (55.9 cm) strip of decorative fabric (optional)

what you do

1. Measure your child's waist and subtract 1 inch (2.5 cm) from the total. (Note: 20 inches [50.8 cm] seems to work for most babies.) Cut the elastic to this length. Overlap the ends by ½ inch (1.3 cm) and secure them with a box stitch (figure 1).

2. Cut the tulle into strips 1½ to 2 inches (3.8 to 5.1 cm) wide and 20 to 26 inches (50.8 to 66 cm) long, depending on how long you'd like the skirt to be. (The strips will be tied in half, so a 20-inch [50.8 cm] strip will result in a 10-inch-long [25.4 cm] tutu.)

3. Slip the elastic onto your leg to make it easy to hold, and tie the strips of tulle around the elastic, making sure the knot is in the middle of the tulle. Crowd the knots slightly (figure 2). Trim any strips that appear uneven or too long.

figure 1

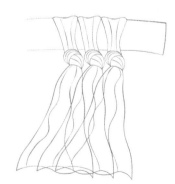

figure 2

designer: **Stacy Dinkel**

4. To make the optional sash, cut 60 to 70 inches (152.4 to 177.8 cm) of the wide satin ribbon. Fold it in half lengthwise, tuck in the ends, and stitch the halves together.

5. To embellish the sash, cut a strip of fabric thinner than the ribbon—in this case, 1½ inches (3.8 cm) wide—and not quite as long as the waistline measurement. Press the edges of the fabric under ¼ inch (6 mm) on all sides and position the fabric in the center front of the ribbon. (Adding fabric only to the waistband avoids the extra bulk that would prevent the ribbon from tying nicely.) Topstitch the fabric in place.

6. Locate the center front of the sash and pin about 3 inches (7.6 cm) on either side of the center point of the elasticized waistband. *Don't* attach it all the way around. Just make a 6-inch (15.2 cm) seam on the top and bottom edges of the sash, following the existing stitch lines of the embellishment fabric, and backstitch at the beginning and end of both seams.

MAKE THE SLIPPERS

what you need

Sewing Kit (page 15)

¼ yard (22.9 cm) of cotton fabric for the tops and linings of the booties

Scraps of synthetic suede or chamois for the soles

¼ yard (22.9 cm) of medium-weight fusible web

Assorted fabric scraps

10 inches (25.4 cm) of bias tape

18 inches (45.7 cm) of ¼-inch (6 mm) elastic

seam allowance

³⁄₁₆ inch (5 mm) unless otherwise noted

pattern pieces

top

sole

heel

what you do

1. Cut out the following pattern pieces:

- 2 tops and 2 top linings
- 2 soles (flip the pattern piece over to get opposite sole pattern)
- 2 heels and 2 heel linings

2. Add fusible interfacing to each piece, with the exception of the soles. On the linings for the top, mark the ¼-inch (6 mm) openings for the elastic, and open each slot with a seam ripper (figure 1).

3. Make the patchwork by choosing eight to 10 fabric scraps in different patterns and colors. Cut strips 1 inch (2.5 cm) wide and 1 to 2 inches (2.5 to 5.1 cm) long. Press them and arrange them as desired. Stitch them to one of the top pieces, overlapping them in straight lines (see figure 1 on page 105) and backstitching at both ends to secure the seam. Turn the top over and trim off any over-hanging ends. Do the same for the other slipper.

4. To complete the tops, place a top liner on the back side of each patchwork top and encase the straight edge of the top and the liner in bias tape (page 27). Be sure to place the narrower width on the right (top) side. Stitch the tape in place.

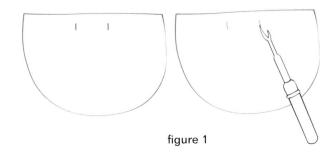

figure 1

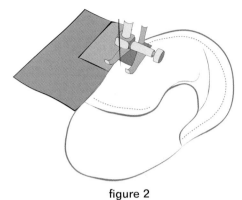

figure 2

figure 3

figure 4

figure 5

5. Fold each top and sole in half lengthwise and mark a dot at the center of the toe on each one. **Note:** Remember to create both left- and right-foot slippers by flipping one sole over to the opposite side. Line up the dots of a top and a sole, right sides together. Beginning at the center point, ease stitch around one side of the slipper. Return to the center and ease stitch around the other side of the slipper (figure 2).

6. Pin each heel piece and heel lining right sides together and stitch a seam along the top edge of the heel. Also stitch along each side of the heel, but leave a ⅝-inch (1.6 cm) opening near the top seam as shown (figure 3). Turn the pieces right side out and press.

7. Stitch a ⅝-inch (1.6 cm) seam along the top of the heel piece to create a channel for the elastic. Use a safety pin to thread 8 inches (20.3 cm) of elastic through the channel you've just created. As you did for the toes, mark the center back of each heel and sole. Line up these points, right sides together, and ease stitch around each side of the slipper (figure 4).

8. Once the slippers have been assembled, run a continuous stitch line around the sole seams. Double check that all fabric layers are securely sewn into the seams. Clip the seam allowance.

9. For each slipper, use a safety pin to thread one end of the elastic through both of the slits you made in the top lining. Pull both ends of the elastic together to adjust the ankle opening. Cut off the excess elastic, overlap the ends, and stitch across them a few times. For neatness, adjust the elastic to tuck the stitched ends into the fabric casing (figure 5). Turn the slippers right side out.

They're a patch made in heaven!

MAKE THE BIB

what you need

Sewing Kit (page 15)

¼ yard (22.9 cm) of cotton fabric, diaper cloth, terry cloth, flannel, or linen

Assorted fabric scraps

8 inches (20.3 cm) of ¼-inch (6 mm) double-fold bias tape

4 inches (10.2 cm) of cord elastic

1 decorative button

seam allowance

³⁄₁₆ inch (5 mm) unless otherwise noted

what you do

1. Enlarge the template on page 125 and cut out two bib tops, two bib pockets, and one embellishment tab out of fabric.

2. Make the patchwork by choosing eight to 10 fabric scraps in different patterns and colors. Cut strips 1 inch (2.5 cm) wide and 2 to 3 inches (5.1 to 7.6 cm) long. Press them and arrange them as desired. Stitch them to one of the bib pocket pieces, overlapping them in straight lines (figure 1) and backstitching at both ends to secure the seam. Turn the pocket piece over and trim off any overhanging ends.

3. To finish the pocket, cover the back side of the patchwork pocket with the second pocket piece. Encase the top edge of the pocket in double-fold bias tape (page 27). Be sure to place the narrower width on the right (top) side. Stitch the tape in place.

4. Lay the tab embellishment right side up on the right side of the bib, and stitch across the straight end. Do this on both bib pieces. Cut 3½ inches (8.9 cm) of elastic cord, then double it over and tie the loose ends with a knot. Lay out the pocket on one of the bib tops with the elastic loop positioned as shown (figure 2). (If you don't want to make an elastic loop, you can use hook-and-loop tape instead, install a snap, or even make a buttonhole.)

5. Pin the second bib top to the pieces, right sides facing. Stitch the perimeter of the bib, leaving a 3-inch (7.6 cm) opening on one side or the bottom. Trim and clip the seam allowances (page 000) and turn the bib right side out through the opening.

6. Press the bib, turning in the edges of the opening to align with the seam. Close the opening and finish the bib by edgestitching (page 19) all around the bib. Attach the cutest button you can find.

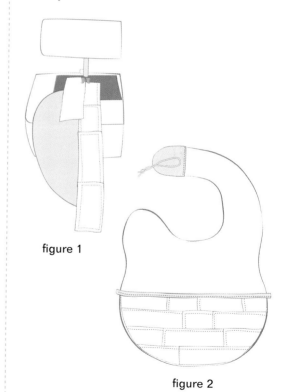

figure 1

figure 2

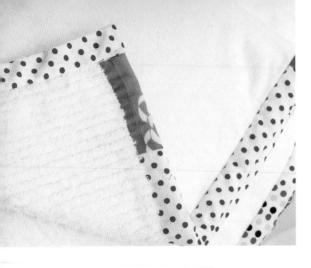

best friends

What's cuter than a baby? A baby with a playful puppy! All it takes is a vintage pattern to embroider on cuddly fleece.

what you need

Sewing Kit (page 15)

1 yard (91.4 cm) of cotton flannel for the front

1 yard (91.4 cm) of chenille fabric for the back

Embroidery transfer pattern of your choice

¼ yard (22.9 cm) combined of fabric scraps at least 2½ inches (6.4 cm) wide, for the binding

Embroidery hoop and floss

seam allowance

¼ inch (6 mm)

finished size

32 x 36 inches (81.3 x 91.4 cm)

designer: **Jessie Senese**

what you do

1. Cut a 32 x 36-inch (81.3 x 91.4 cm) rectangle from both the flannel and the chenille fabrics.

2. Lay the piece of cotton flannel flat, right side facing up. Position the embroidery pattern in a corner of the fabric, leaving about 3 inches (7.6 cm) of margin on the sides. Transfer the pattern according to the package instructions.

3. Using the hoop, a needle, and embroidery floss, embroider the design onto the flannel.

4. With the finished embroidered side of the flannel facing up, lay the chenille fabric on top of the flannel, right side facing down. Pin the rectangles together around the edges. Stitch around the perimeter, leaving an opening of 6 inches (15.2 cm) on one side. Clip the corners (page 20) and turn the blankie right side out through the opening. Fold under and pin the raw edges of the opening to align with the sewn seam. Press the entire blankie flat.

5. Topstitch all the way around the blankie, closing the opening in the process.

6. Cut the scraps into strips 2½ inches (6.4 cm) wide. For variety and interest, make them different lengths—anywhere between 3 and 9 inches (7.6 and 22.9 cm) long. Sew them all together to form one long piece of binding, and press the strip flat (page 27). Fold and press the strip so it's double folded (page 27), and bind the edges of the blanket, mitering the corners (page 22).

So, Baby, what's your pooch's name?

bath hoodie

Yay! Bath time just got more fun. After soap and splashing, wrap Baby in a plush hooded towel with cheerful dots and trim. The best part? This is one item your little one won't soon outgrow.

what you need

Sewing Kit (page 15)

1 yard (91.4 cm) of terry cloth fabric

¼ yard (22.9 cm) of fabric A for the appliquéd circles

¼ yard (22.9 cm) of fabric B for the appliquéd circles

⅛ yard (11.4 cm) of fabric C for the appliquéd circles

¾ yard (68.6 cm) of fabric D for the appliquéd circles and the binding

finished size

36 inches (91.4 cm) square

designer: **Rebeka Lambert**

what you do

1. Cut a 36-inch (91.4 cm) square from the terry cloth. Using the leftover piece, cut a triangle for the hood measuring 18 inches (45.7 cm) long by 9 inches (22.9 cm) high. It's helpful to use a corner of the towel as a guide.

2. Enlarge the circle templates on page 127 and cut out the following circles with pinking shears:

• 6 large circles from fabric A

• 6 large circles from fabric B

• 7 medium circles from fabric C

• 7 small circles from fabric D

3. Randomly place the circles on the terry cloth, including two or three on the hood piece. Let some of the circles hang off the edge of the terry cloth. Pin each circle in place and trim off any excess circle fabric hanging off the terry cloth. Attach the circles to the terry cloth using a zigzag stitch on the outer edge of each circle.

4. To make the binding, cut five strips 2 inches (5.1 cm) wide from fabric D. Stitch them end to end to make one strip about 6 yards (5.5 m) long, then fold and press the strip (page 27).

5. Bind the long edge of the triangular piece that will serve as the hood. With wrong sides facing, place the hood onto one corner of the terry cloth square wrong sides together (figure 1). Pin.

6. Bind the outer edge of the towel, mitering the corners (page 27).

Start filling the tub—it's bath time!

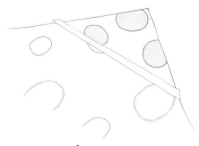

figure 1

crib notes

Baby your baby with a specially monogrammed quilt and pillow set.
Tucked in to sleep, your tot will be bundled in quilted layers of love
and have the sweetest dreams ever.

what you need

Sewing Kit (page 15)

For the quilt

¾ yard (68.6 cm) of fabric A

1¾ yards (1.6 m) of fabric B

⅔ yard (61 cm) of fabric C

1 yard (91.4 cm) of fabric D

1¼ yards (1.1 m) of fusible fleece

For the pillow

¼ yard (22.9 cm) of fabric A

½ yard (45.7 cm) of fabric B

⅛ yard (11.4 cm) of fabric C

½ yard (45.7 cm) of fabric D

12 x 16-inch (30.5 x 40.6 cm) pillow form

Paper-backed fusible web

seam allowance

¼ inch (6 mm)

finished sizes

quilt, 45 inches (114.3 cm) square

pillow, 11½ x 16 inches (29.2 x 40.6 cm)

designer: **Rebeka Lambert**

what you do

1. For the quilt, cut out the pieces using the following measurements:

- **Fabric A:** four strips measuring 4½ x 22½ inches (11.4 x 57.2 cm)

- **Fabric B:** four strips measuring 2½ x 22½ inches (6.4 x 57.2 cm)

- **Fabric C:** four strips measuring 5½ x 22½ inches (14 x 57.2 cm)

- **Fabric D:** four strips measuring 11½ x 22½ inches (29.2 x 57.2 cm)

For the pillow, cut out the pieces using the following measurements:

- **Fabric A:** one strip measuring 3½ x 12½ inches (8.9 x 31.8 cm)

- **Fabric B:** one strip measuring 2½ x 12½ inches (6.4 x 31.8 cm)

- **Fabric C:** one strip measuring 4½ x 12½ inches (11.4 x 31.8 cm)

- **Fabric D:** one strip measuring 7½ x 12½ inches (19 x 31.8 cm)

2. Assemble four blocks for the quilt and one block for the pillow by stitching the pieces together as shown (figure 1). Stitch each strip with right sides facing. Press the seams on the back to one side.

3. Enlarge the letter "b" templates on page 121, or create templates of your own with the letter of your choice. Trace them onto the paper side of the fusible web. Cut the pieces out, leaving about 1 inch (2.5 cm) around the edges of the tracings. Following the manufacturer's instructions, fuse the web to the wrong side of the leftover fabric A and cut out the letters.

figure 1

On the quilt, select one of the blocks and position the letter in the lower right corner of fabric D. Leave a margin of 2½ inches (6.4 cm) on the right and 4 inches (10.2 cm) on the bottom. For the pillow, do the same, but leave a margin of 2½ inches (6.4 cm) on the right and the bottom. Adhere the letters to the fabrics with fusible web and reinforce around the edges with a zigzag stitch.

4. To complete the pillow, cut two pieces for the backing from fabric B: one 12½ inches (31.8 cm) square and the other 12½ x 6½ inches (31.8 x 16.5 cm). On each piece, hem one 12½-inch (31.8 cm) side by folding it over ¼ inch (6 mm) twice and stitching the edge. Assemble the backing as shown in figure 2, placing it right side down on the right side of the pillow front with the two hemmed edges overlapping. Stitch around all sides of the pillow. Clip the corners (page 20) and flip the pillow right side out through the envelope opening in the back. Insert the pillow form.

5. For the quilt front, stitch the four blocks together as shown in figure 3. It helps to stitch the blocks together in pairs, forming two rows, then to stitch the two rows together.

6. Cut a 44-inch (111.8 cm) square for the backing from fabric B, and another square of the same size from the fusible fleece. With an iron, fuse the fleece to the wrong side of the backing according to the manufacturer's instructions.

7. Lay the backing on top of the quilt top, right sides together, lining up all the edges. Pin in place. Stitch around all sides of the quilt, leaving a 6-inch (15.2 cm) opening on one side. Trim the seam allowances, clip the corners, and turn the quilt right side out. Press the seam allowance under at the opening, lining it up with the seam. Pin the opening shut and topstitch around the perimeter of the quilt ¼ inch (6 mm) from the edge, stitching the opening closed. Secure the fabric by stitching along either side of each quilt block seam.

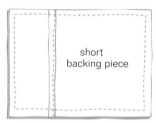

short backing piece

figure 2

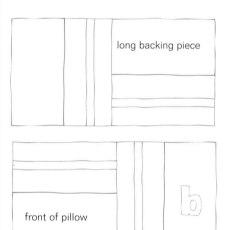

long backing piece

front of pillow

b

figure 3

cutie burpies

Face it: babies are cute but messy. No reason they can't be stylish, though. These burp cloths are made from the softest cotton and terry cloth, and they can double as washcloths or protect clothes at the changing table.

what you need

Sewing Kit (page 15)

11 x 16-inch (27.9 x 40.6 cm) piece of cotton fabric

11 x 16-inch (27.9 x 40.6 cm) piece of terry cloth

seam allowance

¼ inch (6 mm)

finished size

10½ x 15½ inches (26.7 x 39.4 cm)

designer: **Jessie Senese**

what you do

1. With right sides together, pin the two pieces of fabric together. Stitch around the perimeter, leaving a 3-inch (7.6 cm) opening. Turn the piece right side out through the opening, and push out the corners using a chopstick or other implement.

2. Fold the unstitched area under to line up with the seam, and iron it flat. Topstitch around the entire perimeter.

Okay, Baby, I've tossed the burp cloth over my shoulder: do your thing.

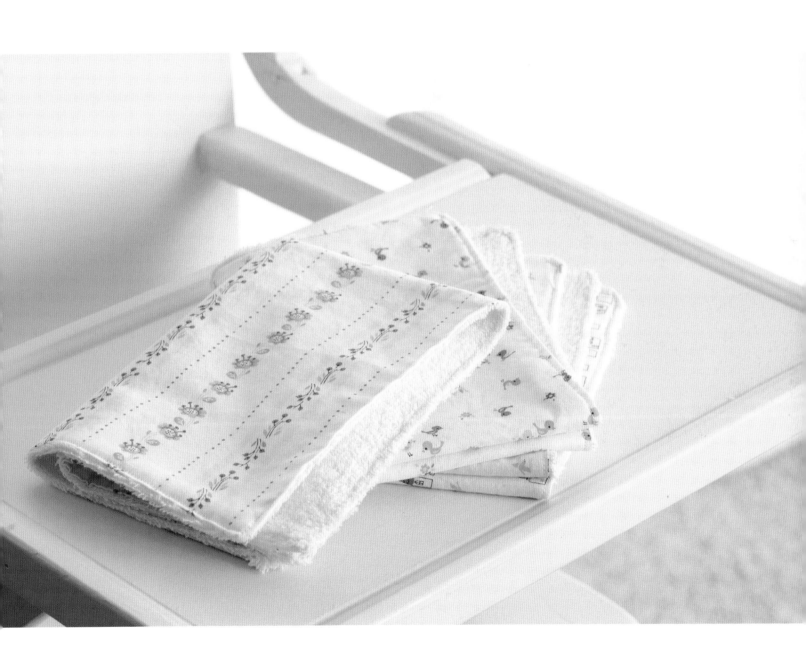

fuzzy wuzzy

Swaddle your little cub in style by wrapping Baby up in the teddy bear hug of this super-soft receiving blanket. One side is made of fake fur and it's backed with a cotton print.

what you need

Sewing Kit (page 15)

½ to 1 yard (45.7 to 91.4 cm) of fleece, depending on the width of the fabric

1 yard (91.4 cm) of cotton print fabric for the backing and the binding

seam allowance

½ inch (1.3 cm)

finished size

24 x 30 inches (61 x 76.2 cm)

designer: **Wendi Gratz**

what you do

1. Cut a 24 x 30-inch (61 x 76.2 cm) rectangle out of each piece of fabric, using scissors rather than a rotary cutter (page 15).

2. Make the binding by cutting strips 2¼ inches (5.7 cm) wide from the backing fabric, joining them to make a piece 3½ yards (3.2 m) long, as described on page 27. That's long enough to go all the way around the blanket, plus an extra 18 inches (45.7 cm). Don't skimp on the extra—you'll need it to miter the corners, and you don't want to end up short. **Note:** If you don't want to make your own binding, use two packages of commercial ½-inch (1.3 cm) double-fold bias tape instead.

3. Lay out the backing right side down. Lay the fuzzy fleece right side up on top of it. Pin the binding strip in place, mitering the corners as you go (page 27). Smooth the furry fleece so that it's tucked under the binding strip.

4. Stitch the binding, and await cold temperatures with anticipation.

cuddle quilt

Once upon a time, someone made a special quilt for the whole family to cherish. Let that someone be you. This is the blankie Baby will want to take along everywhere.

what you need

Sewing Kit (page 15)

3 x 18-inch (7.6 x 38.1 cm) strips of 32 different coordinating cotton fabrics

36 x 48-inch (91.4 x 121.9 cm) piece of chenille fabric

36 x 48-inch (91.4 x 121.9 cm) piece of cotton quilt batting

½ yard (45.7 cm) of fabric for binding

Rotary cutter, mat, and clear quilting ruler

seam allowance

¼ inch (6 mm)

finished size

33 x 45 inches (83.8 x 114.3 cm)

designer: **Jessie Senese**

what you do

1. Use a rotary cutter, ruler, and mat to cut the 32 fabric strips into 192 precise 3-inch (7.6 cm) squares.

2. Pair up the squares, right sides together. Chain stitch all pairs: stitch them one after the other without lifting up your needle (figure 1). When all the pairs are stitched, trim the tails between them, open them up, and press them flat.

3. Next, match each pair with another pair to make a line of four squares. With right sides together, chain stitch the pairs into groups of four. Trim and press again, as in step 2. You should have 48 sets, each four squares long.

4. Match each set of four with another set to make a line of eight squares. With right sides together, chain stitch again. You should have 24 sets of eight squares.

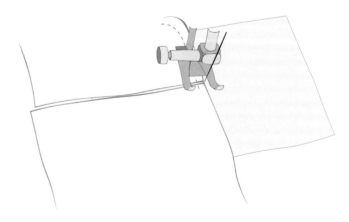

figure 1

5. Lay the strips out on the floor or a large table, arranging them as desired. Stitch the chains into four quadrants. In other words, stitch six strips together at a time, from the upper left, upper right, lower left, and lower right. Press the quadrants.

6. Lay out the quadrants as desired, then stitch them together. The quilt top is now complete.

7. With the right side facing down, lay the chenille backing material on a flat surface. Place the batting on top of it, followed by the quilt top, right side facing up. Beginning in the middle and working your way to the outer edges of the quilt, pin all three layers together.

8. Beginning in the center of the quilt, stitch in the ditch. To do so, follow the lines already created by the seams that join the squares on the quilt top. You don't need to stitch every seam; just do enough to make certain the quilt layers are secure and won't shift. Remove the pins and trim any backing or batting that extends beyond the quilt top.

9. Cut 2½-inch (6.4 cm) strips from the fabric selected for the binding. Stitch them together to form one long piece of binding and press it flat. Bind the edges of the quilt as described on page 27.

You ready for a snooze, Baby?

templates

quilted bib, page 72

enlarge 200%

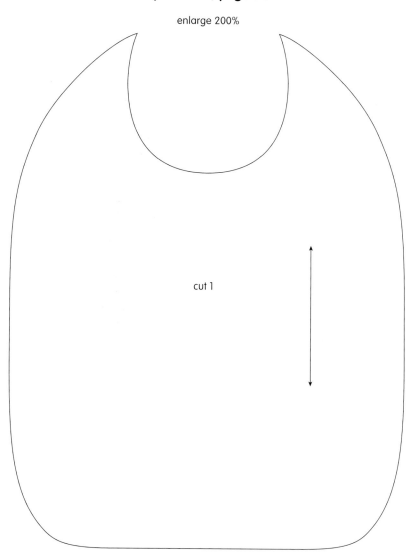

cut 1

crib notes, page 110

enlarge 400%

pillow appliqué

cut 1

quilt appliqué

cut 1

bunny baby, page 78

enlarge 200%

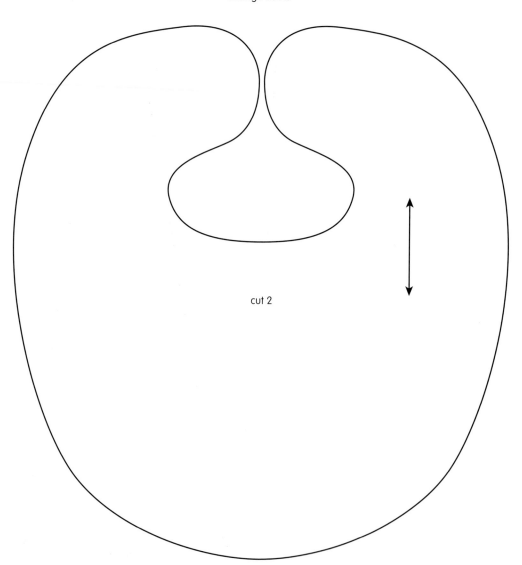

cut 2

on the town, page 68

do not enlarge

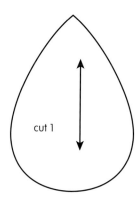

cut 1

necklace appliqué pendant

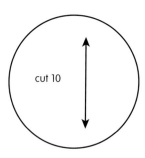

cut 10

necklace appliqué beads

on the town, page 68

enlarge 200%

do not enlarge

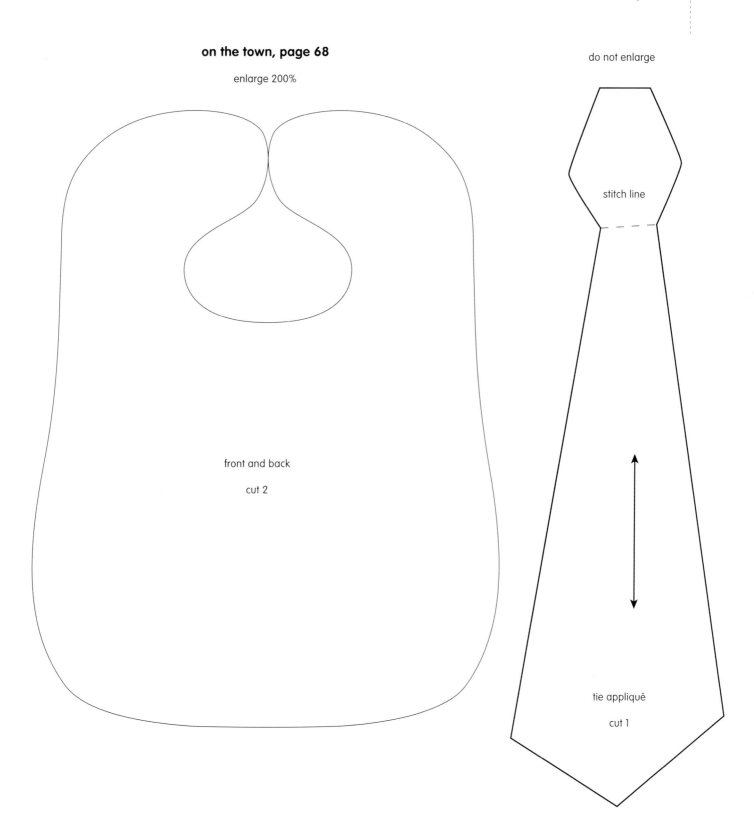

front and back

cut 2

stitch line

tie appliqué

cut 1

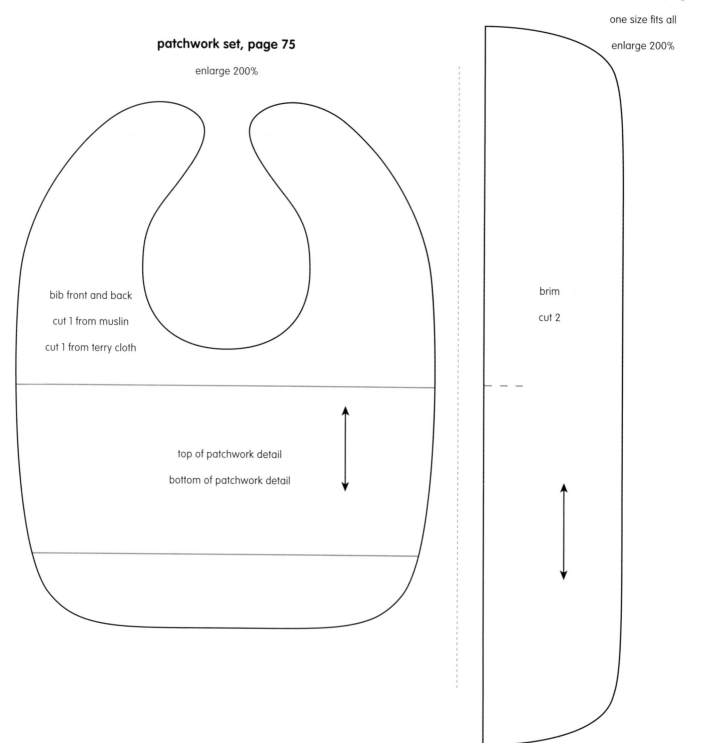

patchwork set, page 75

enlarge 200%

bib front and back

cut 1 from muslin

cut 1 from terry cloth

top of patchwork detail

bottom of patchwork detail

prairie bonnet, page 65

one size fits all

enlarge 200%

brim

cut 2

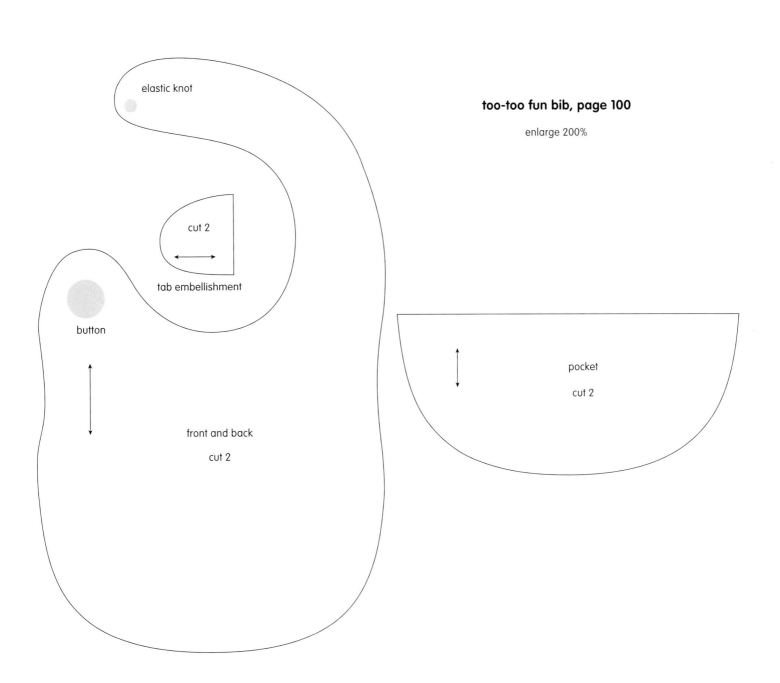

elastic knot

too-too fun bib, page 100

enlarge 200%

cut 2

tab embellishment

button

pocket

cut 2

front and back

cut 2

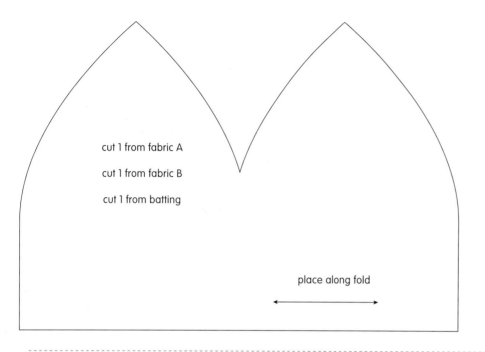

hold me cloche, page 62

size large

enlarge 200%

to alter size after enlarging template, see page 9

cut 1 from fabric A

cut 1 from fabric B

cut 1 from batting

place along fold

ring around, page 89

enlarge 200%

cut 2 of each size

bath hoodie, page 108

enlarge 200%

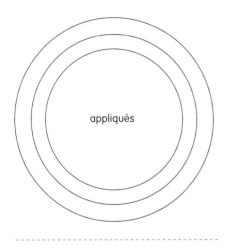

appliqués

no-knit hat, page 49

enlarge 200%

flower

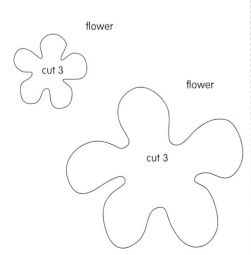

cut 3

flower

cut 3

plushy pocket, page 70

enlarge 200%

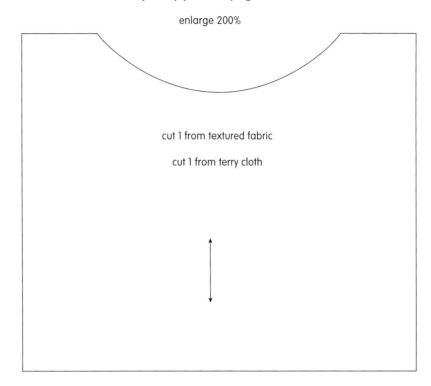

cut 1 from textured fabric

cut 1 from terry cloth

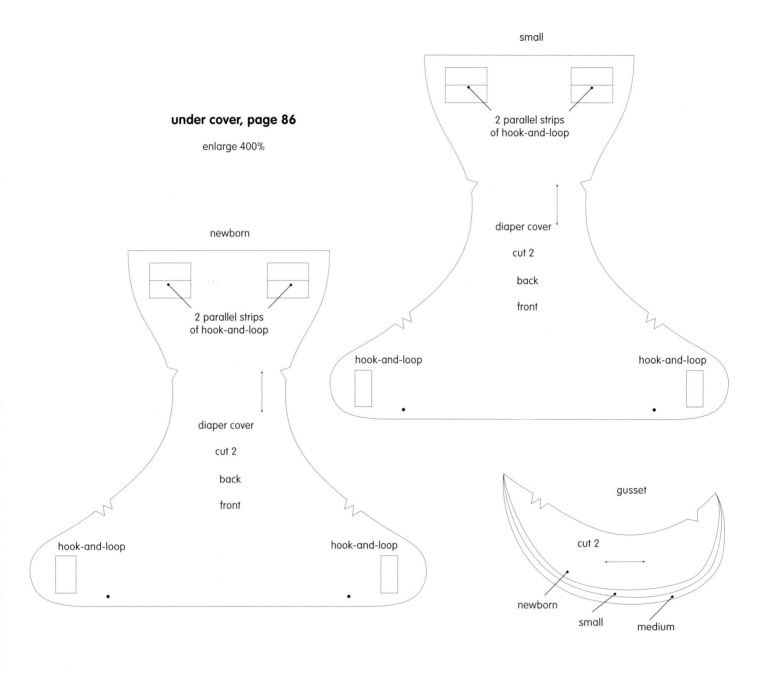

under cover, page 86

enlarge 400%

small

2 parallel strips
of hook-and-loop

diaper cover

cut 2

back

front

hook-and-loop

hook-and-loop

newborn

2 parallel strips
of hook-and-loop

diaper cover

cut 2

back

front

hook-and-loop

hook-and-loop

gusset

cut 2

newborn

small

medium

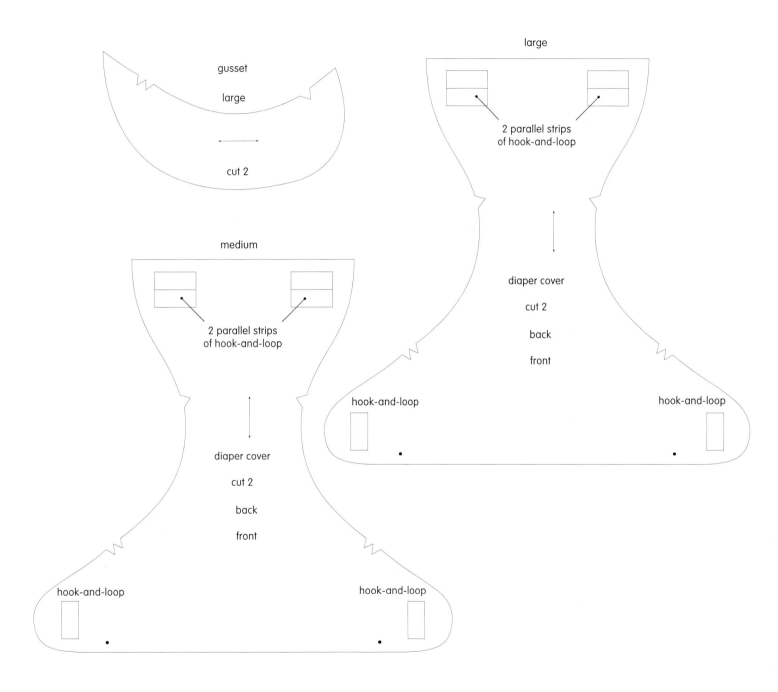

gusset

large

cut 2

large

2 parallel strips
of hook-and-loop

diaper cover

cut 2

back

front

hook-and-loop

hook-and-loop

medium

2 parallel strips
of hook-and-loop

diaper cover

cut 2

back

front

hook-and-loop

hook-and-loop

about the designers

Katherine Accettura is an indie designer and seamstress who sews every day. After sewing and selling small book bag purses called "Pursonalities," Katherine moved on to piecing baby quilts with the help of her mother and giving them away as shower gifts. After realizing how much she loved to make miniature things, Katherine began making baby accessories. She gets great joy from making other people—especially babies—warm and comfy.

Katherine lives in southern Illinois and is wrapping up a bachelor's degree in graphic design at Southern Illinois University. She sells items at www.KatEyez.etsy.com and www.KatEyezCo.com. She loves feedback, so drop her a line at kateyez62707@yahoo.com.

Belinda Andresson is based in Sydney, Australia. She designs and handcrafts a unique range of contemporary patchwork cushions and accessories sold under the label tuttifruiti. Each piece is individually conceptualized and handcrafted by Belinda from her beachside home. She injects a contemporary look into patchwork by pairing bold graphic prints with luxurious wool fabrics. Her creations are not only a feast for the eyes, but a tactile experience as well. Belinda rarely duplicates her designs, making each piece truly one-of-a-kind. tuttifruiti is sold at a number of retail stores in Australia, as well as online at www.modamuse.com.

Stacy Dinkel is the creator of Doodle Factory, items born as a shared effort with her daughter and available in seven boutiques and her Etsy shop, http://MamasDoodles.etsy.com. She's an at-home mama, a part-time social worker, and a woman with a lot of pent-up creativity. Twin degrees in fine arts and counseling have made her realize that keeping her spirit alive requires being artful, as well as helping her hone her skills as an artist. Stacy explores interior decorating, sewing, repurposing furniture and clothing, painting, and photography. She blogs about life experiences and her creative endeavors at http://mamasdoodles.blogspot.com.

Suzie Fry finds time to craft and blog in between working, mothering, cooking, and gardening. She caught the sewing and knitting bugs from her mother and grandmother and started making her own clothes as a teenager. In the many years since, she has expanded her repertoire of crafts skills whenever there has been a brain to pick, a group to join, or a class to take. Her love of things handmade has been fuelled by a growing uneasiness over mass production, consumption, and disposability. Having kids focused Suzie on making smaller-scale things, ones easy to squeeze into a busy, unpredictable schedule, portable and quickly packed away from grabbing little hands. She wanted to make toys for her children that would last, be practical, and be imaginative… but most of all that would be loved. Read about her adventures at www.soozs.blogspot.com.

African-born artist and fabric designer **Tina Givens** injects her art and design with a colorful personality that springs from a broad cultural background and love of life. An enterprising, busy entrepreneur and mom of three, Tina launched Cid Pear, a successful stationery collection, in 2004. Her eclectic style and sense of color has proven to be an irresistible combination.

Working in a nontraditional method of detailed, saturated watercolor painting, Tina creates unique characters and patterns to produce on an appealing product range of textiles, clothing, and gifts. She has also created fabrics for Westminster Fibers. She resides in Raleigh, North Carolina.

Wendi Gratz lives with her family and her sewing machine just down the road from the Penland School of Crafts in western North Carolina. In high school she skipped home ec in favor of wood and metal shop, and she didn't learn to use a sewing machine until college. Her first project was a badly made tablecloth; she learned a lot from that disastrous experience. Her second project was designing and making all the costumes for a play. Now she makes fun clothes, funky dolls, and all kinds of quilts. You can see her work at www.wendigratz.com.

Rebeka Lambert lives with her husband and three young children on the outskirts of Baton Rouge, Louisiana. She received her bachelor's degree from Louisiana State University in 1997. She currently works in information technology,

though she hopes one day to fulfill her dream of creating and designing full time. Her favorite things to make are bags and purses.

After putting crafting on hold during the early years of motherhood, Rebeka is back crafting full force. The discovery of blogs, particularly craft blogs, led her back to it. That daily feedback and sharing of ideas keeps her inspired. You can catch a glimpse of her life on her own blog, http://artsycraftybabe.typepad. com. You'll find stories about her family as well as current projects. She also has an etsy shop, www.artsycraftybabe.etsy.com, where she periodically sells her creations.

Joan K. Morris's artistic endeavors have led her down many successful creative paths, including ceramics and costume design for motion pictures. Joan has contributed projects to numerous Lark books, including *Pretty Little Potholders* (2008), *Pretty Little Pincushions* (2007), *Cutting Edge Decoupage* (2007), *Creative Stitching on Paper* (2006), *Exquisite Embellishments for Your Clothes* (2006), *Hip Handbags* (2005), *Gifts for Baby* (2004), *Hardware Style* (2004), and *Beautiful Ribbon Crafts* (2003).

Jessie Senese keeps a package of baby wipes and a coin purse filled with small bills at the ready: a garage sale might be around the next corner, and she likes to be prepared. She can often be found in the crowded stalls of flea markets, thrift stores, and estate sales in search of the vintage fabrics she adores. Working from her at-home studio in the suburbs of Chicago, Jessie uses her ever-expanding collection of vintage materials to create sweet little things for baby and home. Follow her misadventures in craft at www.sweetjessie.com.

Valerie Shrader made a pair of pink culottes when she was eleven and has loved fabric ever since. She's on the staff of Lark Books, and has written and edited many books related to textiles and needlework. Valerie knits every now and then, too, and dreams about making art quilts. Recently, she celebrated her midlife crisis by purchasing three sewing machines in one year.

acknowledgments

The projects in this book were conceived with love and delivered by a group of incredibly talented designers who we simply can't thank enough.

Under the watchful eye of Nancy Wood and Kathleen McCafferty, the manuscript received excellent editorial care. Intern Meghan Warucka helped out with some of the less glamorous aspects of editorial work—and it wasn't changing diapers!

Art director Megan Kirby acted as midwife throughout design and layout, expertly guiding these pages into the world amid much kicking and screaming. Thanks also to Sandra Stambaugh, who helped bring the images to life with her gorgeous photography.

Nest Organics, an organic home store located in downtown Asheville, North Carolina, loaned many of the wonderful accessories in the photos.

Orrin Lundgren created the easy-to-follow templates in the book, and J'aime Allene added the illustrations that grace these pages. Art assistant Jeff Hamilton and interns Nicole Minkin and Will Ketcham babysat the book and kept it smoothly on track.

We're indebted to all the beautiful babies who appear in these pages (and to their proud parents for bringing them into the fold): Aliye Julianne Dillingham, Ayda Dillingham, Sophia Rose Fontanini, Rochely Chayala Gallordo, Bella Glover, Liam Hoelscher, Sacoya Long, Madison C. McRae, Diego Medina Mendez, William Nunan, Sophia Raye Olinger, and Griffin Wilson.

A big thanks to everyone who made this book possible. You've come a long way, baby!

index